WOMEN
AT
HALFTIME

WOMEN AT HALFTIME

Principles for Producing Your Successful Second Half

DEBORAH JOHNSON

DJWorks
Los Angeles

Women At Halftime
Principles For Producing Your Successful Second Half

Copyright © 2019 Deborah Johnson

All rights reserved. No parts of this book may be used or reproduced by any means, graphic, electronic or mechanical, including photocopying, recording, taping, or by any information storage retrieval system without the written permission of the publisher except in the case of brief quotations embodied in critical articles and reviews.

Johnson, Deborah, author

Issued in print and electronic format
ISBN: 978-0-9885879-8-4 (Hardbound)
ISBN: 978-0-9885879-7-7 (Paperback)
ISBN: 978-0-9885879-9-1 (eBook)

Because of the dynamic nature of the Internet, any web addresses or links obtained in this book may have changed since publication and may no longer be valid.

Cover art by Vikiana, © Deborah Johnson • Royalty free photos

Logo ei8htz © Deborah Johnson • Commercial permission

Deborah's photo by Jessica Johnson:
www.JessicaJohnsonPhotography.com

Visit Deborah's websites at:
GoalsForYourLife.com; *DJWorksMusic.com*

Hero Mountain® is a Registered Trademark, All Rights Reserved

Dedicated to

*my parents, who raised me to embrace
every season of my life gracefully and full of faith,
especially at halftime.*

CONTENTS

Acknowledgements		ix
Introduction		xi
Chapter 1	At the Base of Hero Mountain®	1
Chapter 2	Mindsets Cable	7
Chapter 3	Purpose and Passion Cable	25
Chapter 4	Competency Cable	39
Chapter 5	Skills Cable	71
Chapter 6	Habits Cable	93
Chapter 7	Relationships Cable	121
Chapter 8	Reaching Your Summit	139
Index		149
About Deborah		153
Also By Deborah Johnson		155
Endnotes		157

ACKNOWLEDGEMENTS

There are many who have encouraged me, not only in the writing of this book, but in my personal and professional growth. I don't want to miss mentioning anyone, so let me say that I am grateful for many friends who play a role in different areas of my life.

Thank you to Joel and the entire board I'm leading this year as President of the National Speaker's Association, Greater Los Angeles Chapter. You've pushed me in my growth as not only a leader but also as an artist-entrepreneur who loves to create!

For my new friend Haley, who inspired the stage illustration on the front cover, bringing out my experience as a producer. When we spoke, I realized how many times I've been both behind and before the curtain and how the principles of writing a new script provide a consistent thread throughout my message to women.

Thank you to the women who continue to share their heartfelt stories with me. Their stories not only encourage me, but also challenge me as I continue to help other women.

My lifetime small group, Marcia, Peggy, and JoAnne. You keep me praying, laughing, and growing through the stages of child-rearing, grand parenting, and now elder care as we gently usher our own parents along the path toward their heavenly graduation.

A special thank you to Paula, my trusted editor, who has guided me through all my book-writing projects with tremendous care, insight, and expertise. I appreciate you so very much.

Further, heartfelt thanks go to my musician family, who really keep the song alive in my heart and fingers. Jamie, Peggy and Dianne—what would birthdays be like without our celebrations and shared passion for the constant tune running through our lives? For the few students who have hung on for so many years—Sandy,

Natasha and Lily—my heart fills with joy as you continue to express your music in deeper ways.

I won the lottery with amazing parents. As I watch them shuffling instead of running, inhabiting a smaller world, I understand how important faith is. One day, I will no longer hear their sweet voices here on earth, but I am thankful for the hope we share to enter heaven's gates upon life's ultimate graduation. For my dear sisters, Sandy and Linda, who have given of themselves in so many ways for others, you are truly an inspiration to me. I love you dearly.

My own family is at the top of my grateful list. Mike, Dan and Dave, I am so proud and amazed at the men you have become. You are all so different, yet so alike. When we are together, you make me laugh so hard I cry. Jessica, my dear daughter-in-law, you are such a good mommy to those long-awaited glimpses of pink in my life, as you have given me two amazing granddaughters.

Finally Greg, I'm the luckiest woman alive to be married to you. As I saw your tender care for your parents throughout their last years and even hours on this earth, I realized even more the scope of your compassion, humor, and love. As the lines on your face grow deeper, they are mirrored in my own. From our first blind date until now, we have been on an intimate journey together where my love for you has grown deeper and fuller. We have experienced our own rocks and occasional deep valleys, yet we also continue to climb and grow, reaching our own summit on Hero Mountain®.

Yes, I'm the luckiest woman alive.

INTRODUCTION

MY STORY

In 2007, I was finishing a wonderful year in the music business. While still in my forties *(sort of)*, I had successfully filled 1,000-seat auditoriums for solo concerts over a dozen times in twelve months and my 2008 calendar was filling up. Those were exciting days. After spending extensive time and energy—not to mention tons of emotion—I had not only developed a rewarding music career, but I had also successfully launched three sons into young adulthood. In those crucial years, from 2007-2008, my empty nest meant I had crucial time to invest in my career—finally! Life was good.

Then everything changed when the worst financial crisis since the Great Depression hit. Suddenly all that extra cash audiences had been spending on concert tickets evaporated. Performance halls and local auditoriums found it difficult to sell seats. Various venues all cancelled their bookings with me, so by April of 2008, my calendar became suddenly empty. I felt stuck, and my career horizon showed no quick turn-around.

Welcome to my life at half time. With my career path interrupted. I found myself at the base of what I like to call my Hero Mountain®. As I gazed at the climb before me, I knew I needed preparation for some rocky paths ahead. In that process, I saw many other women facing similar challenges.

HALFTIME

So what is halftime? It's that period in the middle of a game where players reassess their first half, then make adjustments for their future success. It is a brief recovery time to refocus on the most critical action points. An effective halftime in a game occurs when it is dedicated exclusively to identifying and counteracting the most disruptive forces to a team or player's success.

Just as there is halftime in sports, most career professionals need time to reflect on critical talking points and disruptive forces in their lives at halftime, too. Those half-time decisions will largely determine one's remaining life path. Will we merely fade into the second half of our lives, operating a tired, outdated strategy, living on autopilot? Or will we successfully reinvent ourselves to ascend to the personal peaks of our own Hero Mountains®? Only those who reach the top can experience and claim the vistas at the peak.

Identifying and counteracting the most disruptive forces is important in Halftime.

THE GAME PLAN

This book is about both reassessing then re-developing a strategy to succeed in life's second half. Like me, many women manage careers, raise kids, satisfy husbands, serve as volunteers, feel their bodies change *(then slip away!)* and fight culture's incessant attempts to make them invisible.

For it happens that one day, women like me suddenly realize the world has changed. Coworkers start calling us *ma'am* and viewing us as irrelevant. Awareness of that change brings with it tugs of urgency. It is a time for reassessment and evaluation, but where do we start?

Women at Halftime are not dead! They still have a tank full of energy and tons of skills, experience, and perspective. However, negative self-talk screams out questions that can tear them down:

- Can I really start over?
- Does anyone still want me?
- How much more can I learn?

- How much longer can I keep myself together before I lose my mind?
- Can I ever be as good as (*insert a colleague's name here*)?

Women at this stage often describe their feelings in the following ways: *Stuck, Lost, Slogging uphill, Completely unsure, Ready, but not ready, Exhausted,* or *Trapped in neutral.* Further, each is fearfully asking, "Am I enough?"

SUMMARIZING THE SOLUTION: CABLES OF SUCCESS

Cables One and Two: Mindset and Purpose

Effectively confronting **negative talk** and **bad mental code** are necessary for a half time effort. An adverse mindset will negate everything else a woman builds as she climbs her personal Hero Mountain®. Remember the 1930s children's story ***The Little Engine that Could***? Its theme is the value of optimism and hard work. The story's signature phrase, "I think I can" first appeared in a 1902 article, then in multiple sermons, stories, and tales until it became part of that memorable book.

Like that little engine, when we climb our Hero Mountains™, we can change that statement "I think I can" to "I know I can!" As in any mountain climbing effort, the climber needs skills and tools to ensure a successful journey. Similarly, as we define our purposes and gather our gear, we are gathering our climbing cables of success. To build our confidence and maintain our enthusiasm, like that little train engine, we need a positive, confident mindset.

These efforts will establish a focused **purpose** that brings a woman new energy. Whether that purpose is to build an existing business, start a new business, or give more time to a worthy cause, that purpose will provide women reasons to wake up enthusiastically each morning. A well-defined purpose or mission, along with a solid plan will be the turbo engine that propels and empowers all the other cables for a successful climb.

Cables Three and Four: Competency and Skills

A careful, honest, impartial evaluation of a woman's **competencies** is another cable of success. Trying to digest the many self-help books on **finding strengths** and **identifying a passion** can be overwhelming, but this process doesn't have to be a long, drawn-out activity. We begin by finding the pattern and Core Common Denominator™ of all we have accomplished so far. Many times it's surprising! Halftime can be an affirming time of life when we understand who we are, matched with what we truly want to pursue.

After we successfully define our core strengths or competencies, acquiring additional **skills** based on those competencies will increase success in our second half. With the increase of technology and artificial intelligence, many economists claim the need for skilled workers will only grow because more automated tasks can be programed, giving individuals a chance to use their higher-value skills. This is great news for us because developing new skills based on our competencies will increase opportunities to work in a field we love.[1]

Cables Five and Six: Habits and Relationships

With our purpose and competencies ascertained, we must develop healthy and consistent **habits** in order to effectively execute a plan. Reinforcing good habits will help us learn new skills effectively and competently while repeating bad habits will only lead to deeper ruts. To repeatedly practice unhelpful strategies that don't work only brings frustration and defeat. However, a well-defined, healthy habit or routine will act as a management tool to bring success.

In order to keep from falling backwards on our ascent to Hero Mountain, we also need a healthy application of the **relationship** cable. Productive, healthy **relationships** feed our energy with

INTRODUCTION

understanding and support for the climb. Even though it's emotionally difficult to implement, we must let go of toxic relationships that tear down our confidence and hold us back from trying new ventures.

This book is an introduction to the essential cables needed to ascend one's Hero Mountain peak. In addition, Hero Mountain® online and live summits provide further training to maximize the climb for both men and women. This book is designed to help readers escalate their journeys, and then serve as a tool to give ongoing reminders to reflect and evaluate what practices to keep or discard and what approaches to adopt in the future.

Are you ready to get started? Let's go!

ONE

At the Base of Hero Mountain®

Change, it sneaks up so gradually that we hardly notice until one morning, we wake to face a strange image in the mirror—not just any mirror—that magnifying mirror mounted on the bathroom wall. While our mind's eye pictures a high-spirited, young woman with vibrant eyes, who's ready to face another day, the image before us requires a squint, then second or third looks.

Are those deepening crow's feet spreading? Are those actually *permanent* bags beneath our eyes? Several splashes of cold water cannot rinse away the creases around our mouths that have deepened from smile lines to fissures. We lift sagging cheeks to produce a momentary youthful expression. But wasn't it just yesterday that we were nominated for college homecoming queen?

Gray hairs betray us too. We love our mothers, but we don't want to look like them yet because they are older than we are! However our aging faces reflect a maturity of their own. These realizations alarm us.

OUR WORLD IS CHANGING

It's one thing to *look* old and another to *feel* old. Yet at work, a competent career woman in mid-life may notice that the new employees and younger talent at the company, are beginning to tell her what to do. Some have good ideas, yet their methods and management styles are making the older woman feel isolated and irrelevant. She wonders if she should just retire or just hang on a few years more. What else could she do at her life stage? She actually starts *feeling* like she can't keep up. Is this what "old" feels like?

These mid-life shifts bring biological changes, too, that may beget night sweats, hot flashes, pudgy waists, and stubborn pounds. Midlife women may feel like the last runners in a race, trying to stay ahead of the support vehicles, but even then, unable to keep up. At home, as her children leave the family nest, bedtime stories, school activities, needy teenagers, and other mom duties are no longer required. Who needs women like them at this stage when the forties turn to fifties and beyond?

Welcome to halftime.

HAIRPIN TURNS

In order to thrive in mid-life, women must get ready for sudden changes as well as gradual ones. Some can be like those hairpin turns in Stelvio Pass in the Alps of Northern Italy. At an elevation of 2757m (9,045 ft.), it's the highest paved pass in the Eastern Alps and the second highest in the Alps with forty-eight hairpin turns. Similarly, Alpe d'Huez in the Western French Alps, with twenty-one hairpin turns at an 8.1% grade, hosts the Tour de France cycle race, testing the athletes' skill and agility.[2]

Near our home is Mt. Baldy, a mountain in Southern California whose roads share the length and steepness of Alpe d'Huez. Like those Alpine peaks, in fact, the last few miles of a Mt. Baldy climb are quite steep. I have personally experienced the tight switchbacks at the crest of Mt. Baldy Road. Further, I have attended and performed at the sobering memorial services for those unfortunate ones who misjudged those sharp mountain turns and plunged to their deaths down Baldy's steep cliffs.

We don't have to stay on a road of hairpin turns.

We may feel like we're on a road with forty-eight hairpin turns like Stelvio Pass, the steep grade of Alpe d'Huez or even the tight switchbacks of Mt. Baldy. To remain on a treacherous course like those means taking drastic turns to change direction. If we don't fall off a steep cliff on our way, we will eventually reach our destination.

That route may be okay for those motivated and intrigued by the challenges of steep windy roads. However, for women at midlife who have twenty years or more to be productive, traveling on a steep road with hairpin twists is not the optimal choice. Climbing to a new place in life doesn't have to be a difficult journey or even a long one. We can choose a different path.

There is more than one way to scale a mountain. That's where the beauty of climbing cables come in to assist us, making the climb manageable. Think ski resorts. There, gondolas take skiers to the summit with little disruption and much less effort. That's the kind of support we may need to make a successful life transition.

There is more than one way to scale a mountain.

THE BEAUTY OF CABLES

Take gondolas, for instance. The Gulmarg Gondola in Gulmarg, India, is known as the world's highest cable car. The actual cable moving the gondola is 40.5 mm thick, almost two inches in diameter, and it ascends to 13,000 feet, similar in scale to the California's Mount Whitney at 14,500 feet.

Another example is the gondola at California's Mammoth Mountain, one of North America's largest ski areas, that rises to

11,000 feet. Obviously, it is easier to ride to the heights of Mammoth Mountain than to hike one of its trails to the top. I know from experience since I have ridden the Mammoth gondola and biked down its steep slopes on the other side. *(Mainly to prove to our sons that I could do it!)* Because the narrow, steep path down had twists and turns, I took some good tumbles. Yet I would not have attempted the ride at all if I had to first hike up the hill.

Some cables help us climb while others give us a change of scene. Many theatres also contain cables, known as theatrical rigging systems or fly systems, which include a system of ropes, blocks and counterweights. Most larger systems are electronic, but many older theatres still have manual rigging where a person pulls on the rope or cable to raise and lower scenic backdrops.

So in the same way that a stage has different sets or scenes, our lives have different backdrops or chapters. When I was producing my original musicals on theatrical stages, one of the larger old theatres had a rope to draw the curtain and change scenes, which takes extra effort and strength to manage. Likewise, it may take additional work to raise and lower a new backdrop, curtain, or scene during different life stages. Regardless of a half-time woman's current backdrop, she can still choose how to climb her personal Hero Mountain.

In the same way that a stage has different sets or scenes, our life has different backdrops or chapters.

DANGERS OF DOING NOTHING

If a woman were told she had cancer today, what would she do? Depending on the diagnosis, she has many choices, ranging from aggressive treatment to doing nothing. However, her doing nothing doesn't make sense with today's medical and naturopathic options. At the very least, a proper and specific assessment should be made, followed by strategic decisions and treatment implementation. In the same way, a **proper assessment** of where we are at midlife or halftime is the first step before applying defined principles to our life direction.

Consider half time during a sports game. Coaches don't waste those sessions by discussing non-essentials. The team doesn't decide to quit or keep executing the same ineffective plays. Instead, after a brief reassessment, the team focuses on the most critical strategies with minor adjustments to help the players make a comeback to win the game. That process of reassessment and strategic adjustment is the focus of this book.

When feeling defeated, focus on the most critical strategies to make minor adjustments.

As we look in that mirror again, we acknowledge that we are encountering a wonderful time of life because we have more skills, experience, and capacity than at any other stage. Today, new avenues of opportunity abound for recreating and renewing a life path or career. With the proper tools, guidance, and support, we can produce a difference not only for ourselves, but for others.

SHORT TERM REMEDIES

Before running hysterically to our local Botox clinic or cosmetic center in search of a short-term remedy for aging, we should reconsider. Why can't we wear those deepening lines and grey strands with pride? They are gainfully earned, infused with successes as well as missteps. After all, we have earned those smile lines! There's no need to discount our outer appearance. As the saying goes, *If the house needs painting, paint it*, but we shouldn't exaggerate or distort our outer appearance. Instead we must grow in appreciation of the various colors we hold inside!

Don't exaggerate your outer personal paint job. Instead, grow in appreciation of the various colors you hold inside!

No matter one's skin color, education, or language, each woman is beautiful. Therefore, she should feel empowered, taking the time and energy necessary to re-strategize for the next chapter of life. It is unnecessary to take the difficult road with multiple switchbacks and steep, rocky hills. There are helpful cables and even fly systems available to ensure a much smoother climb.

The goal is to reach one's personal peak as quickly as possible. Our own peak is a destination uniquely different than the countless other voices clamoring for attention. With any ascent, it's important to focus on our own ascent, and not on others climbing around us. Destructive plunges occur when we get distracted and take our eyes off our personal journey and goals. So we must not become consumed with others but keep ourselves focused on the goal, reaching the summit of our Hero Mountain.

Don't be distracted by others but
keep focused on the goal, to reach the
summit of our Hero Mountain.

TWO

MINDSETS CABLE

The Mindset Cable creates stability for all the other cables. If it is weak or cut, the chances of reaching the summit are greatly diminished or even negated. This is a cable that is important to adjust and strengthen through the decades of life just as mountain climbers develop determined mindsets before embarking on an arduous ascent. That mindset keeps them focused on the goal instead of the valley below.

The 1950s comic book television series Superman starred George Reeves in the title role. He was immortalized as a caped hero, flying through the air to save damsels and divert tragedies.

The illusion that Superman could fly was a landmark special effect, leaving the television audience awed at the superhero's ability to soar through the air. However, those early special effects employed rather primitive cabling systems so that Reeves, while suspended, often wobbled along while his legs dangled awkwardly. In fact, during the taping of one *Superman* episode, the wires suspending Reeves suddenly broke. During the fall, the actor escaped a concussion but declared he wouldn't "fly" on those risky cables anymore.

As a result, using the magic of television, the producers devised an alternate way to create the illusion of Superman leaping off buildings. They used a springboard. Without such ingenuity, the series would have halted.³ Not only did they find a new way to simulate take-offs, but they were also able to repurpose the footage they had already filmed, using it repeatedly for various flying scenes. Since the 1950s, animation has advanced greatly, eliminating the need of cables in creating aerial illusions. Yet the principle still rings true: that a broken cable could have completely shut down production.

*If the mindset cable is weak or cut,
the chance of climbers reaching the summit
are greatly diminished or even negated.*

BAGGAGE, NEGATIVITY AND FEAR

Mont Blanc, the largest peak in Europe, is one of the world's archetypal mountains. While its panoramic view is beautiful, its iconic ski lift is one of the world's most dangerous. For example, the gondola cable on Mont Blanc snapped in two, when January storm Eleanor ripped through France in 2018. At 12,000 feet, winds whipped up to 155 mph (250 kph), causing a buildup of heavy frost and ice on the cable system.⁴ When a cable like Mont Blanc's, spanning 3.1 miles, is under pressure from the elements, it's easy to understand the danger.

Similarly, our personal mindset cables are often in danger of being loaded down with icy baggage, frosty negativity, and subzero fear. Life's circumstances may cause our support systems to snap unless they are checked, reinforced, and cleaned periodically.

*If the mindset cable is loaded down with icy
baggage and frosty negativity and subzero fear,
life's circumstances may cause our support
systems to snap unless they are checked.*

BIKING AND MINDSETS

I love taking a relaxing bike ride. However, I have not fully embraced clipping in with my bike shoe, often required on a mountain or road bike. Will I be able to stop or control my bike if I'm clipped in? This fear of mine derives from a false premise.

Clipped-in bike shoes do not lessen my ability to control my ride. In fact, I have experienced success many times with clip-ins during my cycle class at the gym. *(Yes, I know that's different!)* Even though I ride a stationary bike in that situation, I have found my clip-in shoes release with a simple foot twist.

Once I mastered the concept of clipping into the bike pedals, I could concentrate on working the gears. Shifting gears on a bike is an entirely different task than using clip-in shoes. When I owned my first ten-speed, *(Does that date me?)*, I had to learn to shift gears while riding. Graduating from my stingray banana seat bike *(That does date me!)* to a ten-speed offered greater speed and momentum. Even though I did not always access the gears optimally, downshifting when climbing a hill made my ride easier. Also, my ten-speed allowed me to keep up with my girlfriend down the street, as together, we rode our bikes to school.

Just as clipped-in shoes and shifting gears improve a bike ride, a positive, flexible mindset aides one in transitioning into different life stages. Having the proper mindset serves as an assistance cable on the mountain climb. Our full attention is required as we hike or bike up our personal Hero Mountain®. Just as pedaling makes a bike move, the right mindset will affect a life direction. We shift gears to re-strategize and re-group just as bikers downshift to accommodate a topographical change.

Just as pedaling makes a bike move,
the right mindset will affect a life direction.

INGREDIENTS FOR SUCCESS

On Sunday mornings, I make pancakes from scratch. One week, I forgot to add the baking powder, so the pancakes came out flat and dry. The omission of that one little ingredient, only a half tablespoon, negatively affected all the batter. That baking error reminded me that having the necessary ingredients is required for my success.

In a similar way, it takes a series of mountain climbing cables to scale the mountain of career change. All of them are necessary, even the seemingly insignificant ones. Therefore, we can't limit our upcoming prospects and dreams with a mindset of negative self-talk.

A mindset is an attitude, a mental state, an approach or inclination. A woman at midlife can approach life's topographic changes with a zeal and willingness to repurpose her abilities or stumble along a path of pessimism and desperation that weighs her down. It's a midlife choice all must make. If a biker is not prepared mentally for her mountain ride, she will feel like she's perched on a precipice thirty stories high. The view alone, whether real or imagined, can bring a quickened pulse, followed by panic and stress.

Discerning reality and changing perspective can bring clarity to such a scary scene. For instance, there is often a well-worn trail on the mountainside. It's just a matter of following it to the next destination. In the same way, discerning what's real and having confidence in one's long-term experience may actually bring enjoyment and the thrill of the next challenge. However, the mindset that holds many back from attempting their climb or ride is negative thinking, or head trash.

Discerning what's real with confidence in one's long-term experience brings enjoyment with the next challenge.

THE DANGER OF HEAD TRASH

Head trash can be the lies we believe or the negative script that pervades our thoughts. The resulting panic or fear can impede our momentum and frustrate our goals. Those negative thoughts keep us "stuck." Their range is unlimited:

- It's no use being creative because I can't leave this stupid job.
- I can't give this project my best effort because it won't work out.
- Technology is moving too fast for me.
- No one needs the skills I possess.
- I've failed so many times, why try again?
- I won't make enough money to survive if I change careers.
- My friends and family will think I'm crazy if I try something new.

How does a woman get beyond such persistent head trash? First, she realizes that some negative thoughts and feelings act as healthy warning signs. So she cannot discount every adverse reaction. Stepping out on a new venture may sound terrifically exciting, yet ominously intimidating. Making a change requires women to develop realistic expectations and use logic *(not just emotion)* to create and implement a viable career or business plan. Such strategies silence negativity and fear. The implementation of a sensible and skillfully crafted action plan brings confidence.

Some negative thoughts and feelings act as
healthy warning signs.

Preparation is key, illustrated by the legendary college sportscaster Keith Jackson, who passed away at age 89 in January 2018. He once gave the greatest advice of his career to Steve Raible, a fellow radio commentator and news anchor: "Don't be the guy they have to prop up; always be prepared." Jackson obviously followed his own advice as he kept his job for over three decades, thriving in an unpredictable field. Like Jackson, we can't be prepared for every roadblock, but we can formulate a solid plan that anticipates future barriers.[5]

TRAPPINGS OF COMPARISON

Defining realistic expectations with a solid plan takes thought, courage and many times help from trusted colleagues and experts. The head trash of unhealthy negative self-talk is then greeted with confidence and hope for the future.

> *We can't limit our upcoming prospects and dreams with negative self-talk.*

Another aspect of head trash is the trap of comparisons, especially on social media. Measuring ourselves by the standards posed on a colleague's Facebook page or Instagram post often brings feelings of worthlessness or inadequacy. Such traps send us off course, but it is possible to change the language we speak and the way we think to keep us on track. It's important to speak truth to ourselves and discard artificial standards of success.

VICTIM MENTALITY

Another impediment to successful change is the **victim mentality** or **defeatist thinking**. A person seized by a victim mentality focuses on life's disparities and then feeds on them. With today's social media climate and more organizations asserting rights for various ethnic, social, gender or professional groups, nurturing and displaying a victim attitude has become a badge of honor, regardless of the facts.

However, adopting a victim attitude can actually bring destruction to both individuals and organizations. It creates a short circuit that stunts personal growth. To test whether we have fallen into the victim trap, we can evaluate ourselves through the following assessment:[6]

Step One: Do I sweat the small stuff?

Victims note all slights no matter how insignificant. If the barista who didn't make a woman's latté extra hot or if the espresso maker failed to ask the customer for her exact preference, then these servers must be judging her negatively.

If colleagues look at her without smiling, then they must be assessing her weight gain or criticizing her height. If they *don't* look at her or say hello, they must hold some deep-seated bias against her and all other people like her. What about her hair color, her skin color or her intelligence? They're judging her!

Everyday incidents like these lead to faulty conclusions that make victims feel angry, bitter, and vengeful. Then paranoia sets in. After all, critics with periscopic eyes really are out to get such victims and make their lives as miserable as possible.

Step Two: Do I keep a record of perceived slights or aggressions and review them consistently?

Victims keep journals to document any possible slight or insult from the day. It helps them relive each pain and increase their victim awareness. Such venting fuels angst and resentment so that situations become exaggerated in their minds, and their bitterness grows into a desire for revenge.

Further, such victims expand on each entry and express all their feelings, whether angry, bitter, or vengeful. Every slight is processed as a personal attack and act of discrimination. They view their exaggeration not as evil but as vital.

Step Three: Do I maintain a top-ten list of offenses against me?

To remain victims, individuals compose lists of the severest assaults against them. The items on their offenses list may change and grow in magnitude throughout the years, leading to the next stage—martyrdom.

Step Four: Do I routinely market martyrdom in well-rehearsed speeches?

Like the elevator pitch *(a ten-second speech one can recite at a moment's notice)*, victims craft a talk that details their victimhood. Each sentence begins with "I" or "my" because victims have no room for pronouns like "we" or "you." Adding a hash tag for each item on the list effectively enhances its seriousness on social media. These martyrs' speeches need to be all about them. Otherwise, how will people know how much they suffer?

Step Five: Do I post my top-ten list as a reminder of life's injustices?

Dedicated victims keep their list of top ten offenses ever before them, replaying past events and conversations in their minds and placing the items on mirrors, closet doors, refrigerators, or even computer monitors. Posting recent injuries online is also effective. Posts heighten their victimized status and draw in other disconsolate souls, creating a social media buzz!

Step Six: Do I practice looking and sounding like a victim?

True victims do not forget or forgive. Instead they develop instant recall to recount their personal history of maltreatment. With practice, they take on the body language of victimhood with hunched shoulders, downcast eyes, and furrowed brows. Further, victims practice speaking in a whining or defiant tone to add credibility to their victim profile.

OPTIMIZED AND CHAMPIONSHIP MENTALITY

This assessment list is meant to be somewhat satirical, of course, but it should also provoke our examination of victimization. Can you see how immobilizing this kind of negative self-talk can be? Some of the angst we face at halftime is often self-inflicted, so that demands from us an honest confrontation. Many women remain stuck after halftime because they advance their victimhood persona.

The contrast to a victim mentality is a championship mentality. Shaun White, Olympic Gold Medal Snowboarder in the 2018 South Korea Olympics, had a nasty crash four months before the games. He was in New Zealand on a training run and smashed his face on the lip of a halfpipe, requiring sixty-two stitches, along with a pulmonary lung contusion. During recovery, he asked himself some important questions.

"Do I really want this?" he thought, sucking for air. "Am I pushing something I don't need?" He decided to get back on his snowboard, even though he has constant reminders of the crash.[7] His confidence was initially crushed almost as much as his body.

On the other side of the crash and of the Olympics, White feels stronger than he ever has been before, but the biggest hurdle he's had to clear has been mental: "I feel more like I know who I am and I know my riding and my abilities," he said. "It's just kind of a mental mindset, having won and then having to win after winning—which is always a great problem to have." In other words, winning mentally is just as important as winning on the slope. Finding motivation and drive have been a challenge he has faced again and again. Yet a dynamic, flexible mindset that helps to adjust, move, and change has been his key to moving forward.

White admits that when he was younger, he possessed an undeniable fire: "It was easy to show up rain or shine." But as he ages, his life gets more complex with a dog at home and relatives calling: "You've got to push those things aside and focus on the goals ahead."[8]

*A dynamic, championship mindset and approach
prepare us to adjust, move and change.*

A HEALTHY MINDSET

A healthy mindset doesn't just consist of a Pollyanna smile while ignoring or denying negative thoughts or feelings. Certainly, discounting our emotions insures that problems will surface in undesirable and unhealthy ways and that brings increased stress.

A tire blowout is a good illustration of what happens with escalated stress. With a sudden flat, the driver feels the panic involved in seeking a safe place to pull over on the highway. This panic and its ensuing adrenalin rush may produce undesirable or impetuous actions, like swerving too quickly or causing an accident. Similarly, an eruption in one's life can manifest itself in unhealthy habits, bringing on toxic relationships, anger, bitterness, and even emotional meltdowns.

Rather than panic, it is important for a woman to identify her true feelings, then actually write them down. Those feelings that leave us disquieted, agitated, or discouraged are real, so it's important to have a channel to express them. However, with each entry, the addition of positive self-talk including **thankfulness, humor,** and a willingness to **learn** will take us off the difficult, often destructive, switchback roads caused by head trash.

*Positive self-talk including thankfulness, humor and
willingness to learn will take us off difficult,
often destructive, switchback roads caused by head trash.*

Mindset of Thankfulness

As an anecdote to negative thinking and reactionary panic, we can keep a gratitude journal or a blessings list. It's important to focus on simple pleasures and note how we are grateful, several times a day; then repeat. Simple pleasures can include the smell of morning coffee, personal freedoms, the majesty of the mountains, a simple rose on a desk, or devices that save time. As Aristotle said, "We are what we repeatedly do. Excellence, then, is not an act, but a habit." Make a habit of focusing on life's simple pleasures.[9]

Philip Simmons, English professor and widely published author of fiction and literary criticism, was just thirty-five years old in 1993 when he learned that he had ALS, or Lou Gehrig's disease, a fatal neuromuscular condition that usually kills its victims in two to five years. With two young children, he suddenly had to say goodbye. By learning the art of dying, he succeeded against the odds, in learning the art of living. He died in 2002 at age forty-five. He described his routine in his book *Learning to Fall*:

> Each day that I can get out of bed in the morning, I am blessed. Each day that any of us can move our limbs to do the world's work, we are blessed. And if limbs wither, and speech fails, we are still blessed. So long as this heart beats, I am blessed, for it is our human work, it is our human duty, finally, to rise each day in the face of loss, to rise in the face of grief, of debility, of pain, to move as the turtle moves, her empty nest behind her, her labor come to nothing, up out of the pit and toward the next season's doing.[10]

Simmons shared those thoughts nine years after his ALS diagnosis. Even though he was dying, he wrote about living despite, "A degenerative illness bent on emptying me out one teaspoon at a time."

Like Simmons, we can uncover areas of life to add to our blessed list. Nothing is too insignificant or inconsequential for gratitude. Then every day as we get out of bed, we review our blessed list with a **grateful heart,** replaying the positive language we have created. That affirmative discourse is a significant step in combatting the mental negative code that can easily overtake us.

Mindset of Laughter

The iconic late-night talk show host Johnny Carson scoured the *Los Angeles Times* every morning, mining fodder for his humorous *Tonight Show* monologues. If Carson could run a comedy show on bits from the *L.A. Times,* we, too, can find a lot to laugh about. We can also develop the ability to laugh at ourselves.

Real-life stories are often the most humorous, absurd, or comical. Dr. Lee Berk, Associate Professor at Loma Linda University, is a pioneer in mirthful or laughter research. He and his team found the **hormone system benefited from laugher**. It reduces blood levels of the detrimental stress hormones cortisol and epinephrine. Surprisingly, when those stress hormones are reduced, numerous immune system components can re-optimize and regain normal function.[11]

Laughter can actually boost the immune system! Berk's team found that the part of the body with the most receptors for neuropeptides of emotion is not the brain, but the **gut**. There is a very intimate communication between emotion and the gut—which is the largest immune organ.

Laughter has the power to boost the immune system.

So the next time we burst out laughing, we should pay attention to our bodies—specifically the lower belly. It moves! In fact, when I instruct singers how to breathe, I have them take a breath expanding the lower belly while keeping the shoulders level and relaxed. This type of breathing gives a vocalist the essential support required to execute a musical phrase effectively.

Proper breathing and relaxation also extend vocal health and longevity, which makes a tremendous difference in many musical careers. Experiencing healthy laughter will do the same for anyone, relieving stress and connecting the body with the brain, which can fend off those useless feelings of martyrdom.

Mindset of Learning

In addition to thankfulness and laughter, a commitment to **lifelong learning** pulls us out of mundane routines that trample our confidence and morale. The value of increased knowledge and perspective serve to melt away obstacles and irresolvable issues. The benefit of a lifelong learning attitude not only provides for the present, but for the future. Many studies document the benefit of keeping the mind active to curtail symptoms of dementia and Alzheimer's. Likewise, many tout the benefit of puzzles or learning to play an instrument as a way to stave off cognitive deterioration.

However, the stacks of Sudoku puzzle books we found after my father-in-law passed was telling. Sadly these puzzles didn't postpone his cognitive deterioration. However, the combination of physical exercise, healthy eating, mental stimulus and a positive outlook can prolong a healthy mindset and lifestyle.

Reading, taking classes, discovering new hobbies, and even starting a new business are mentally stimulating. With different learning styles, including visual, auditory, reading/writing and kinesthetic/physical, we are not limited to one approach. There are many short online surveys to help a woman determine her specific learning styles if she doesn't already know! The guiding principle is to find what will stimulate thoughts within our interests; then we can find new pursuits as lifelong learners.

> *The combination of physical exercise, healthy eating, mental stimulus and a positive outlook can prolong a healthy mindset and lifestyle.*

HALFTIME BRAIN

Hormones play a role in a woman's mindset when approaching halftime. Just as many women experience the first *mommy-brain* symptoms long before they actually conceive a child, many may experience *halftime-brain* as they approach midlife. As with the *mommy-brain* transformation, the *halftime-brain* has the potential to override even the most career-oriented woman's circuits, changing what she thinks, feels, and values.[12]

One of the most apparent symptoms of this shift at midlife often materializes in a desire to chuck everything and everyone and start life over. A menopausal woman is less worried about pleasing and caring for children or a spouse. It is now time to expand her horizons and opportunities on a grander scale. Mid-life can rush down like a waterfall, leaving women less worried about impressing others. As estrogen levels decrease, the hair-trigger circuits in the amygdala that rapidly altered a woman's reality right before her period lesson, *(sometimes pushing her to see bleakness that wasn't there or to hear an insult that wasn't intended)* giving her a more level emotional state.[13] Her middle-aged brain is a more certain, steady machine.

The ironic news is the *halftime-brain* is less susceptible in some ways to head trash than it was prior to menopause. Mid-life women often find themselves less worried about impressing anyone.

These processes are like electrical systems. For example, in my old kitchen, a circuit would blow at the most inopportune time. These disruptions turned my Belgian waffles into a soggy and gooey mess, a true frustration for any cook. But once I remodeled my kitchen and upgraded my electrical system, my circuits became reliable. In the same way, if we could see the connections inside the *halftime-brain*, we would observe that the circuits between the amygdala *(the emotional processor)*, and the prefrontal cortex *(the emotion assessment and judgment area)* are fully functional and consistent. They are no longer easily over-amped and short circuited at certain times of the month. That's one blessing of menopause.

It's a deliberate choice to develop a healthy mindset during halftime.

The renewal of reliable brain circuits is great news for most women. Even though there are other bodily changes occurring, it is entirely possible to develop a healthy mindset with a positive attitude during halftime. However, that transition to positive thinking requires a deliberate choice.

As with many of life's issues, women must make purposeful decisions about their futures. We can either keep treading in stagnant water or reassess and implement a renewed attitude and fervor to grow, learn and change. A healthy mindset combats the futility of a sluggish and sedentary second half. Thankfulness, laughter and a lifelong learning desire serve to scrape and clean icy cables that could easily snap. A positive mental outlook will help us climb our Hero Mountains successfully!

APPLICATION

Do you feel there is anything close to snapping or breaking in your life? If so, name it. *(Examples: stress from a high-pressure job, toxic relationship, financial difficulty)*

1 _____
2 _____
3 _____

Name an area where you assume, rehearse and practice a victim mentality. *(Examples: blaming others, unresolved anger, woe-is-me attitude.)*

_____
_____

How will you develop an attitude of thankfulness? List three things right now you are thankful for.

_____
_____

How can you add laughter to your life? Note at least one idea.

_____
_____

What will you do to engage in lifelong learning? Write down a couple subjects you secretly long to explore.

_____
_____

MINDSETS CABLE

In the following boxes, define some of the hormonal changes you are experiencing *(or have experienced)* and the healthy mindsets you will apply.

HORMONAL CHANGES	HEALTHY MINDSET

THREE

PURPOSE AND PASSION CABLE

In order for purpose and passion to be valuable contributors on the ascent up Hero Mountain, it is extremely helpful to articulate in written form both a **purpose statement** and a **mission statement**. These statements assert two distinctly important goals about your life and your proposed venture. The purpose statement will clearly define "what" one intends to bring to the market and accomplish. The mission statement articulates "why" one is passionate about those goals. We will work through both at the end of the chapter but first, explore the nature and value of both statements as illustrated by climbing ropes.

There are two types of ropes for climbing: **dynamic** and **static**. (*Similar to dynamic and static code, written about in the book **Bad Code!**)*[14] Dynamic ropes stretch to absorb the impact of a falling climber. In contrast, static ropes have little stretch making them efficient for ascending a rope, for emergencies in lowering an injured climber, or hauling up a load. Lengths and weights of ropes vary according to the type of climb and use.

In the same way, well-written purpose and mission statements are structured with enough stability to hold the weight of solid goals and dreams. At the same time, they are flexible enough to withstand the stress of the emergency "change of plans" that life and competition inevitably throw our way. A clear purpose, equipped with dynamic and static understanding will prepare us to successfully execute an ascent up Hero Mountain.

Once, on a beautiful California day, I inhaled the scents of freshly-cut grass and bare soil across rolling hills, dotted with fresh blooms. Crystal skies framed the surrounding mountains. While the view proved spectacular, the occasion remained bittersweet, as I stood at my cousin's graveside to bid her farewell. A life without purpose had been wasted—lost too soon.

My cousin Sherry and I, similar in age and interests, shared many girlhood moments during our school years. In high school, clad in glittery costumes, she had twirled a gleaming baton, her thick blonde hair waving as she led the band. I envied her as I practiced on my unadorned grand piano in the early morning—all alone. Later on, Sherry worked in the Los Angeles garment district where I loved to explore the sample-size racks of well-crafted clothes with her, in search of a fashion treasure. To me, Sherry's life appeared so exciting. She sparkled in those stylish clothes that matched her personality.

Later on, while attending a university in Los Angeles, I often dropped by to visit her. At first, she greeted me with her quick smile and small talk. However, as the years passed, she met my greetings with glassy eyes and detached responses; her once thick, blond hair had grown stringy and thin. In her apartment, as E.L.O. played on a turntable, she spoke dreamily of the music and the man she'd met who took good care of her.

In the months that followed, Sherry increasingly isolated herself from family and friends, and slowly skidded, then succumbed to drug addiction. One tragic day, her landlord discovered her lifeless body in her apartment; she had died alone with only her cat for comfort.

What happened to the sparkly baton twirler? Her untimely death made me search for answers on how such a tragic loss could come to someone in our family, a young woman once so full of excitement.

One difference I noted between her life and mine was aspiration fueled by a clear purpose.

Ambition, driven by a clear purpose, is central to achieving goals because it equips us to create well-defined objectives. This is especially true in the second half of life. A well-defined goal keeps one focused and provides immediate feedback when distracted. Equally as important, a clearly stated purpose contributes to healthy habits and a schedule that becomes orderly and effective, as it becomes easier to decline unnecessary activities. When purpose is clear, the discipline of lifelong learning feeds that purpose.

I had teachers and coaches training me as a concert pianist and vocalist because my parents encouraged my progress and development. Had no one guided Sherry by helping her find answers to life's important questions? Had she faced her personal demons alone?

Drugs rip a life apart, as the next fix becomes the main ambition for the addict. However, drugs alone didn't cause Sherry to end her life. Her demise began before her addiction, for she had no career design, no life purpose, no end goal in mind. With prudent counsel, guidance, and a commitment to a plan, her life may have yielded different results with focus, direction and promise.

That lack of purpose sent her to an early grave on a green hill with only a small stone to commemorate her brief life. Sherry's story and others like hers fuel my passion to help women learn how to find a clear purpose, establish a goal, chart a course, and find purpose. That is why I am writing this book.

In the same way, well-written purpose and mission statements carry enough flexibility along with stability to hold the weight of solid goals and dreams.

START WITH THE END IN MIND

Young people are often asked, "*What* do you want to be when you grow up?" Yet no one asks the question, "*Where* do you want to be when you grow up?" By where, I don't mean location. I mean "*Where do you want your career to take you?*" It's important to ask both questions, especially at halftime when life positions and aspirations become much more intimately intertwined.

How can a woman define her personal sphere of impact? Ambitions and dreams are admirable. However, what we all must ask is, "What legacy will I leave behind?" When we lose loved ones and must sort through and dispense with their earthly belongings, the stark reality of life's brevity and limitations strikes us. The philosophical question that whispers from life's tapestry is, "*Why* are we here?"

Building memories and constructing work that will last beyond us is noble and worthwhile. However, nothing on earth lasts forever. Even family businesses find it difficult to sustain themselves beyond the third or fourth generation. What begins as a superstructure becomes a shell of what it once was. In fact, only thirty percent of all family-owned businesses survive into the second generation.[15]

> *It's important to ask both questions:*
> *"What do you want to be?"*
> *as well as "Where do you want to be?"*
> *especially at halftime when*
> *life positions and aspirations become*
> *more intimately intertwined.*

OUTDATED OR CLASSIC

Many books, songs, medical finds, and technologies become obsolete quicker than the tap of a touch screen. Those works that last prove their value over time. Songs and books remaining through the centuries contain some universal, unchanging truth. That's why classical music, literature, and art are studied and revered in educational institutions.

Despite their boundless talent and body of work, many classical composers were destitute during their most productive years. Consider, J.S. Bach, for example, who wrote prolifically for both the church and the court during his lifetime. Yet half of his brilliant manuscripts were used as waste paper for wrapping fish. Still Bach lived with purpose, so his brilliant compositions we play today speak of it. His experience, along with that of other artists and composers, shows that wealth and fame don't always signify a life of purpose and passion.

The big questions is, "What is our *why?*" A mere goal or action plan is not the ultimate reason for setting a compass toward a particular direction. Purpose, mission, and vision statements, while entangling and confusing, should be related in message and aim. Our core purpose must combine the *why*, the *what*, and the *where*.

WHY, WHAT, AND WHERE

One of the great principles of comedic humor is to simplify the message, reducing the topic to its core essence. In improvisational comedy, each scene begins with identifying the *who*, *what*, and *where*. If the basic parts are not identified, it is difficult to advance the scene. The basic elements count! So if we find ourselves in one of those scenes where the story lags, we feel frustrated and uncertain, unable to move the scene forward. That stall is what happens when we ignore the basic elements of comedy writing.

Similarly, in writing musicals, composers cut lines and songs that fail to move the story along. For example, when I had to trim superfluous lines and scenes during a world premiere of my musical, I resisted omitting that remarkably clever scene or lyric. Yet clearing that clutter actually created more engaging scenes.

> *Our core purpose should combine
> our why, what, and where.*

THE WHY-MISSION STATEMENT

So let's begin to write our mission statement. In creating a mission statement, the *why* should be one short sentence. That's it! Confusion in crafting mission statements lies in adding extra language that explains the *what*, which is our purpose statement and this muddies the core message. *Why* do we provide value?

To begin, a mission statement is not a job, a role, or a to-do list. Mission must capture our personal passion and define our personal callings; it should not be the reproduction of anyone else's. We are unique, so we establish and define what principle, cause, or purpose we stand for, even if that stand is opposed. That approach eliminates the nonessential clutter to bring clearer focus.

Once we determine what doesn't excite us, we characterize what drives us. A great way to explore this is by asking yourself, "What gets me up in the morning?" Whatever that is, is likely to be driven by our passion. Next, we need to determine *why* it motivates us. We can construct methods and strategies later with vision and goals. Here, it is important to focus on our core motivators. If we created a happiness meter, what would constitute a 10 on that scale?

> *Mission must define our personal callings;*
> *it should not be the reproduction of anyone else's.*

SPOTLIGHT MISSION MOTIVATION

Some eagerly jump out of bed to work for a not-for-profit organization in order to leave the world a better place. For example, many organizations bring clean water to impoverished countries by digging wells. Some associations rescue children from slavery; others fight against drunk driving.

Scholars are another kind of group, driven to focus on education or research to provide tools for better living. Still others are inspired to deliver a service to the market that is unique and helps others live a better life. A mission statement must be clear and consistent with what motivates a woman to move forward. It is the static climbing rope with unchanging support for us, leading the way up Hero Mountain.

Discovering and defining our mission is vital not only in beginning our journey, but in providing unwavering support all the way through. We should give ourselves permission to understand ourselves. Halftime is a tremendous point in life; after all, women at mid-life are not irrelevant. The more options we explore, the less likely we are to feel *stuck*. Here's an example of my mission statement, followed by some broad areas to think about:

> *Driven by the desire to encourage and effectively*
> *equip women for success, we exist to provide women*
> *with all the tools, both technical and mental,*
> *that they will need to enjoy more success in the*
> *second half of their life than they did in their first.*

- Media
- Business
- Food, Art or Entertainment
- Science
- Technology
- Family
- Economics/Personal Finance
- Construction
- Military
- Faith/Religion
- Sports

This basic list is meant to help jumpstart our brains. We then ask "where" our passions are leading us and "why" we think we're designed to pursue a particular course.

Discovering and defining one's mission is an important process.
We can give ourselves permission to understand ourselves.

THE WHAT-PURPOSE STATEMENT

A purpose statement is a value proposition. What value can we give to others through our business or life's work? In this statement, we draw upon experience, skills and strengths to fulfill our mission. It is important and helpful to look at our own life's story and not discount our past.

For example, experience obtained from years being in the music business "gig economy" and the necessary creativity to keep working, both equipped and pushed me to develop a successful business not just dependent upon gigs. Further, even though I've written and produced musicals and traveled the country performing, I've experienced my own head trash of perfectionism and constantly comparing myself to others. Others seem surprised at my feelings of inadequacy and not-good-enough thoughts, especially since I possess a good amount of natural talent and drive.

Over time, I realized that I could use my battles with insecurity and professional obstacles not only to grow personally but also to help others. This is part of my value proposition. I focus on women at halftime because ladies across the country confirm that our experiences are similar. Our shared common challenges coupled with my defined process of accounting and overcoming those challenges is core to the value I bring to the marketplace of ideas. The way this works itself out looks like this:

> *Drawing on both years of experience and the successful implementation of a well-developed business plan and guide, we equip women in every area of their lives to experience success in the second half of life.*

MISSION AND PURPOSE

My mission statement includes equipping and helping women take advantage of technical opportunities. Technical challenges are common at halftime. However, there is a huge demand and opportunity for those who have life experience, or what are currently defined as "soft skills," combined with basic technical knowledge.

To further expand the "why" of my mission statement with the "what" of my purpose statement, I draw on my experience of "learning by necessity." I've struggled and faced frustration with creating video, websites and even computer code. However, I have grown and cultivated learning attitudes using tech, so I want to help others discover and build upon their unique experiences, expanding their tech abilities, too. When other women tell me of their own professional needs to work, even after retirement, I want to help them by sharing what I have learned and developed, not only with how to develop a business, but how to use current technologies to accelerate their success.

THE WHERE-PASSION

Let's go back to the question, "*Where* do you want your career to take you?" Many facing halftime have lost their ability to dream. It's important to give oneself permission to imagine and create even a better second half than the first.

Most would agree that change is important to move forward in life and business. However, change is seldom comfortable or convenient! Change brings disruption, rips us from our comfort zones, and brings violent moves and uncomfortable tension. It's easy to lose hope while we reroute our life paths.

Yet healthy change can bring much good! In adapting, we must let go of fears and discouragement in order to venture forward. This process of letting emotions go can be like conquering an addiction. The appetite for a substance doesn't just disappear like the vapor vanishing from a simmering stew. Even when an addict is free of a harmful substance, the body still craves it, so the brain responds to those emotional triggers. Resisting those triggers brings physical side effects, such as headaches, nausea, or panic attacks.

Unless the triggers are challenged, the craving will return again and again. So how does this relate to us? Charles Duhigg in ***The Power of Habit: Why We Do What We Do in Life and Business***[16] proves in several studies that we can change a habit by replacing that habit with a new, healthy one. The healthy trigger needs to activate a desirable activity or object to replace the undesirable craving. This process is not always pleasant or satisfying, at least at first.

> *Letting go of some of the adverse feelings associated with change will assist in our venture to move forward.*

For example, I felt quite uncomfortable when I committed to migrating my websites from one server to a different server. Even though I had a strong reason for the change, I feared the task before me. I craved my comfortable, safe zone despite my website's limitations and vulnerabilities, like being hacked. Yet I knew change was necessary if I wanted to provide different products and services for my clients and audiences.

The process was not easy. It took longer than I expected. Further, the technical details involved in launching a membership site were extensive. However, I put on my techie hat and got busy, working hard. The result has been a positive, beneficial route for my business direction. I have worn my techie hat long enough to create quality videos and a membership platform that has extensive potential for growth. Also, I launched detailed online learning programs that can produce the residual income I desire.

I love the creative process *(anyone can see this from the dozens of CD albums on my wall!)*. Combining my skills and passion with market trends gives me the energy, strength and courage to make important changes even when those changes take me out of my long established comfort zones. A willingness to change is crucial when crafting a purpose or mission statement. That statement will then serve as a compass.

PURPOSE AND PASSION CABLE

A willingness to change is crucial when crafting a purpose or mission statement.

OUR PURPOSE IS OUR COMPASS

Everyone needs a good sense of direction and a purpose provides a guide. That is why vehicles and phones have directional guidance. Even before Google Maps, Siri, or Alexa, we had Thomas Brothers and Rand McNally maps. Yet to make use of any of these navigational systems, we must determine our cardinal direction, whether north, south, east, or west. In other words, we need a compass, whose magnetized pointer indicates the polarity of the North Pole. It is a precisely measured scale, a universal guide used in construction, in U.S. military operations, and in mining to assist with underground navigation. What is vital to those massive operations is equally vital for us.

> *Taking the time to define our main mission or purpose, along with determining our passion will keep us focused with magnetic guidance for our successful second half.*

If our personal compass is off direction, then our chances for success diminish. Whatever projects, businesses, or even relationships we develop should relate to our mission with precision. All of our defined projects, ventures, and plans relate to our short and long-term goals. Taking the time to define our personal mission, coupled with our personal passion, will keep us focused like a compass' magnetic guidance, leading to a successful second half.

Creatively brainstorming and dreaming about what we want for the future are exciting and stimulating personal projects to complete during halftime. I'm giving permission for us to do just that! Start with the *why*, then proceed by defining the *what* and *where*. Determining one's passion isn't rocket science and doesn't take deep psychological study. *(Although I do know a rocket scientist and can give referrals if needed!*) It only requires reflective time to honestly consider what matters and where we want to go. We cannot discount this step.

No one's life should end like Sherry's. Further, we want to avoid disappointment that comes from pursuing a passionless quest; midlife can be time to chase a lifelong dream. The *how* to fulfill one's purpose comes later with training and tools but defining *what* and *where* has to come first. The *what* is one's purpose and passion. We must define ours now with a strong rope that leads to our summit!

MISSION AND PURPOSE STANDING TOGETHER

Let's compare how mission and purpose stand together. Hypothetically, an emergency room may have as its value proposition "We give assurance to the distressed." Their mission statement could read, "To reflect the noblest of human virtue, we deliver timely emergency services to give assurance to the distressed."

Their purpose statement would further define *what* they do that is different than other ERs that are not that focused. Their purpose would state the actual value they provide that gives them a competitive advantage. This assertion is vital because it provides us with the compelling reason for providing our services.

Ready to give it a try? The application included after this chapter will help to create drafts of both a mission statement and purpose statement. It will help start the process to craft or re-craft a halftime mission and purpose statement for your life and business.

APPLICATION

Think back and list some of the major changes that have occurred in your life during that last 10 years.

Use a little imagination here and describe the following: If you continued learning and gaining experience at your current pace, *who* would you be in 10 years?

Who do you *want* to be in 10 years?

_____

_____

What do you *want* to be in 10 years?

_____

_____

Where do you *want* to be in 10 years?

_____

_____

What FEARS are you facing that could hold you back?
- Fear of the **Future**
- Fear of **Finances**
- Fear of **Relationships**
- Fear of **Incompetence**
- Fear of **Resources** *(including knowing the right people)*
- **Other Fears**

On a scale of 1-10 *(1 being lowest)* how would you rate your present Happiness Meter? Why?

_____

_____

Complete this **Mission Statement Exercise** by filling in the blanks. Think back to the areas we explored earlier and answer *why* you feel driven to make a difference. Don't make this too difficult—this can be simple!

My example: *Driven by the desire to encourage and effectively equip women for success, we exist to provide women with all the tools, both technical and mental, that they will need to enjoy more success in the second half of their life than they did in their first.*

Driven by the desire to _____,
we (I) exist to _____.

Complete this **Purpose Statement Exercise** by filling in the blanks. This answers *what*, including your unique experience.

My example: *Drawing on both years of experience and the successful implementation of a well-developed business plan and guide, we equip women in every area of their lives to experience success in the second half of life.*

Drawing on years of experience in _____,
we (I) _____.

FOUR

COMPETENCY CABLE

Some mountain climbers ascend sheer cliffs without any cables or ropes to aid them. These climbers use other tools that provide a strong, safe grip, such as shoes and carabiners. When speaking about a cable related to competency, we will not only focus on abilities that aid us, like what we are passionate about and what our mission is, but also our personality makeups and current opportunities. In the next chapter we will focus on building skills.

For a climbing example, Tom Cruise, in the opening scene of **Mission: Impossible 2**, performed his own rock-climbing stunts. With just a thin safety cable *(later digitally removed)*, he scaled a vertical cliff bare handed, jumped a huge crevasse, then hung from a rock ledge by his fingertips; that's not my idea of a good time! In the process, Cruise suffered a shoulder injury, but many reviewers felt the authenticity of Cruise doing his own stunts added substance to the film.

The actual filming took place at Dead Horse Point in Utah. Few adventurers climb there without wires, so Cruise was no exception. The film's production team would have preferred to use a stunt double with even more cables for protection. However, Cruise remained committed to performing his own movie stunts, despite the dangers or risks of injury.

For a real-world example, the climber Alex Honnold free-soloed El Sendero Luminoso *(The Shining Path)* in El Portero Chico, Mexico, in a little over three hours. The 2,500-foot climb to the summit of El Toro some consider the most difficult rope-less climb in history. To prepare for the ascent, Honnold and a friend first scaled the mountain wall with cables to clean away every loose rock in their path. Hunnold knew that one slip of the foot or wobbling stone would send him plunging to certain death on a climb with no cables.[17]

During Hunnold's landmark climb, a well thought-out path was first established, much like first comprising both mission and purpose statements. Ultimately he was propelled by his core competencies: strong hands and arms and legs that could endure endless hours of strain and testing. This was built upon a foundation of vast amounts of experience. Unlike Tom Cruise, Hunnold ascended without any safety net or tether. He only wore gripping shoes.

For most climbers, the right equipment is necessary not only for protection but also for enjoyment, increasing the pleasure while lessening the fear. For those wanting to attain "hero" status, the right equipment is vital in order to do what many around them say can't be done.

In the same way that cables are related to mountain climbing, our competency and personality form our own cables that allow us to ascend certain career paths. These characteristics are connected within us in ways that, when understood, greatly increase our capacity to achieve more than when operating unaware of those attributes.

Understanding those connections supports the emotional strand for us so that pressure and stress do not hinder our career climbs. A woman must understand her core strengths and match her assets to her work and passion to create a strong rope or bond that can guide her without risk of a break or failure. Discovering ***core competency and strength*** is the focus of this chapter.

A well-executed climb not only includes great equipment, excellent planning and strategic development, but is fueled by an intense desire to achieve and live out a life of purpose. It also includes developing the planned ascent around strengths and experience while minimizing the effects of weaker abilities.

> *In the same way that cables are related to mountain climbing, our competency and personality form cables that link us to certain career paths.*

DISCOVERING STRENGTHS

In some academic circles, there is intense focus on the difference between competency and strengths. Many refer to strengths as an innate ability that is not learned. Competency is attributed to a natural skill developed from past experience. For our use here, those terms will be interchangeable as strengths and competency are difficult, if not impossible, to distinguish and separate precisely. For women who want to discover their individual strengths, numerous psychology books on personality types, temperaments and individual traits are readily available, like those in the past by Carl Jung, Sigmund Freud, Isabel Briggs Myers, and Katharine Briggs. For a more recent source, I really enjoy the insights from Sally Hogshead's *Fascination System*, defining personality archetypes.[18]

From these resources, we can review the basic concepts in an uncomplicated manner to determine our competencies and core strengths. However, we will use basic competencies as our launching point for expanding possibilities at halftime. Understanding the connection between the common denominators in our aptitudes and interests is just as important as obtaining the right ropes for rock climbing. These insights can hold us up like strong cables in our life's climb. We will be looking at common elements in what we love to do, current skills and competencies, future dreams, aspirations and purpose.

At halftime, the participation in this process is especially relevant because by examining her past experience, coupled with an accurate assessment of her abilities and opportunities, a woman can evaluate the best path to take in pursuit of her mission and purpose. Further, what we once considered "lesser strengths" may have developed through time and experience into more dominate skill sets. Consequently, halftime is a great time to pursue new options and ventures!

> *What we once considered lesser strengths may have developed through time and experience into more dominate skill sets.*

When defining basic personality types, most people are usually some combination of introvert and extravert, depending on the circumstance. A woman can recognize her partialities when she is pursuing differing tasks, like when she wants to take the lead or when she prefers to work alone.

INTROVERTS AND EXTRAVERTS

Introverts love to work with ideas. They value their alone time. In contrast, extraverts like activity happening all around them and enjoy working actively with objects or people.[19] In my case, I am an introvert with an extravert job. I love people but place great value on my alone time, creating.

While I find great fulfillment working quietly, my husband loves the noise of activity. Once on an evening date, he took me to a local bowling alley just to talk. Bowling alleys are not the quietest place for conversation, but that night he needed the "energy" of the noise to fuel him after a long day. From that experience, I recognized his extraverted tendencies, but fortunately, that didn't scare me away.

> *If we are in fields that match our skill sets, we have a vast range of work options to explore.*

Many careers are appropriate for both introverts and extraverts. I used to think that all entertainers or public figures had to be extraverts, but then I encountered many introverts among my performing colleagues. As a result, I then recognized the reserved qualities in my own artist life. This company of introverts include many significant names: J.K. Rowling, (**Harry Potter**), Bill Gates, (Microsoft), Christina Aguilera, (artist), and Courtney Cox (actress).[20] Even Josh Groban, the classical-pop star says, "I don't leave the house much, and when I tour, it gives the small sliver of me that's an extrovert a chance to get out and party."[21]

Both introverts and extraverts have great potential. As long as we work in fields that match our skill sets, a wide range of work options are available to us. Most professionals will experience numerous changes in their career, even while working the same job. Toward the halfway mark, many employees may even gravitate toward positions that would have been unsuitable for them ten or twenty years earlier.[22]

Capability, combined with prior work, strengthens the common cable of competency. Maturity and insight that come from years of experience can make halftime an exciting period to explore new possibilities. The objective is to clarify and simplify the process with fun and insight. To do so, we begin with the climbing metaphor of a carabiner.

THE CARABINER – A CONNECTOR

When rock climbing, a carabiner, part of a fall protection system, is a metal loop with a sprung or screwed gate *(opening)* used to quickly and reversibly connect components like ropes or slings. They operate with the same principle as a heavy-duty safety pin with a tight, locked closure. Heavier carabiners offer a more secure attachment and enhance a climber's peace of mind.

Just as a carabiner connects components, a well-defined core competency connects acquired cables of experience, skill, and opportunity. Disconnection and doubt result when our connections are ill-defined and weak. When there is little or no enthusiasm for ideas, projects or sales presentations, self-doubt, discouragement and fear set in. The "not good enough" language creeps in contributing anxiety and negativity, bringing additional stress. It is important to revisit one's strengths and competency to rebuild confidence and focus.

> *Just as a carabiner connects components, a well-defined core competency connects the cables of experience, skill and future opportunity.*

Healthy Relationships

It's easy to see how fruitless sales efforts and business ventures contribute to frustration and discouragement, but there's another surprising source of hopelessness many suffer from at halftime: relationships. Detachment, augmented by life altering circumstances or strained personal relationships can make a woman easily slide down a rocky slope of discouragement and despair. When her once-close relationships including a family member, business associate, friend or even spouse become strained or broken, it is very difficult to garner the emotional energy to keep climbing to the summit of a personal Hero Mountain. Toxic relationships or friendships are emotionally draining, yet they may be difficult relationships to release and terminate.

Are These Connected?

It is important to first examine connections between hindrances; then move forward. While some are hindered by troubled relationships, others are paralyzed by fear of failure or change. When fear, insecurity, jealousy or any other distraction blur our vision, discovering our strengths becomes difficult. Furthermore, clinging to destructive habits make an individual scared to pursue professional help. Any of those cases can leave women feeling frozen, frightened, or trapped.

With life expectancy now at 78.8 years, there is no reason not to pursue in the remaining two or three decades either a second career or a meaningful mission during life's second half. This is especially true given the aid of healthy lifestyles and the medical advances in our society. The seventy-six million people born between 1946-1964 are now between the ages fifty-four to seventy-two.[23] Many in this baby boomer generation will not have generous pensions when their sixties arrive. The reality is they may be working well into their seventies. There is great value in examining one's core strength and competency to successfully link past strengths and experience with subsequent truly fulfilling opportunity. Understanding this value is important, but also there are essential first steps.

There is great value in examining one's core strength and competency to successfully link past strengths and experience with subsequent truly fulfilling opportunity.

Let's start by reminding ourselves what is hindering us from moving forward, covered in chapter two. Grabbing onto a solid cable with a healthy mindset is essential for maximum effectiveness. This is the time to revisit the mentality it takes for a successful climb.

Then, with a strong carabiner in hand, let's connect within it the cables of past experience, skills and current opportunities that will securely support us. After re-evaluating what is holding us back, it is time to act. These first steps won't get us to the top of Hero Mountain, but will establish the right direction for the climb.

The process of discovering core strength and competency may be hard emotionally, but it need not be difficult. It doesn't require psychoanalysis. In fact, determining the common denominators connecting a life and career should be fun, simple and full of self-discovery, revealed in midlife. So how can we find the common thread woven through many of our activities and work? I propose the Core Common Denominator™ system.

DISCOVERING CORE COMMON DENOMINATORS™

In mathematics, a common denominator is an element that is shared by all numbers. For example three is the common number shared by 6, 9 and 12. If the word *denominator* scares us as a math term, we can think *element!* In fractions, the common denominator of ¼, ⅜ and ⁶⁄₁₆ is four.

For a person, her common denominator is a characteristic or interest shared by all members of a group. For example, local city council members share a deep interest in their community as well as the experience and success with their work in that community. Subsequently, they meet together with similar desires and goals *(common denominators)* to make decisions that will best serve their particular city.

In our pursuit and discovery of core competency or strengths, it is important to identify the shared elements, interests and characteristics in these areas: what we love to do, our current skills, future dreams and our mission and purpose.

> *A common denominator is a characteristic or interest that is shared among inclinations, skills and purpose.*

DISCOVERY EXERCISE: FOUR COLUMNS

To allow us to discover our own personal "common denominators" I've devised a straightforward exercise. Here are the basic steps to identify the necessary connections that illustrate a person's interest, skill and direction: First draw four columns on a sheet of paper. *(See examples and guides at the end of this chapter)* In the **first column**, we define what tasks we absolutely love to do. This list should include multiple items, unless we are grumpy and irritable without enthusiasm for much of anything! Our range of items can encompass a range of activities, such as writing, speaking, gardening, counseling, performing, creating, selling, or teaching. The list can be minimal or extensive.

Make sure some items are artistic as well as recreational. Listing these will unlock the right side of our brains. When we record every type of project we like to do or have done, certain events may also come to mind. For example, assisting a particular kind of client, teaching a class, performing in a stage production, or planting a vegetable garden. Reviewing such events helps us formulate a "love-to-do" list.

After making the "love-to-do" list in the first column, we expand the elements of that column by identifying what we love about each item listed and the reasons why. For example, I love to create new content, whether it's a song, newsletter article, or a book. To expand those elements and answer the "what and why" questions, I imagine the joy or benefit others gain from listening, performing or reading what I create. That insight motivates me to create even more. We will talk more about the expanded elements later.

Next, the **second column** is for listing current skills. What can we do? These skills may include tasks as simple as typing a Word document or as involved as creating code for a new application. We can also be creative in this column. What feels *easy* to master? We do not have to be an expert in one particular field. This column can also include something we have experienced in the past, lying dormant for some years. *(What about those piano lessons?)* However, with a little time and focus, could we resurrect a buried skill or awaken a neglected talent?

Do not discount soft skills. Most think of skills as specific and teachable abilities that can be measured. However, soft skills are less tangible. Soft skills are personal attributes that enable someone to interact effectively and harmoniously with other people. According to research by the Hay Group division of Korn Ferry advisory firm, women score higher than men on nearly all emotional intelligence competencies, which are soft skills.[24]

There are many different models of emotional intelligence, focusing on different abilities and assessments. The focus of this book is not to delve deeply into those models, but give an overview to help identify core competencies. Here we will speak of the main four domains: self-awareness, self-management, social awareness and relational management. Within those four domains are the twelve emotional intelligence competencies,[25] defined by Goldman and Boyatzis in the book Primal Leadership.[26] They are:

- Emotional self-awareness
- Emotional self-control
- Adaptability
- Achievement orientation
- Positive outlook
- Empathy
- Organizational awareness
- Influence
- Coach and Mentor
- Conflict management
- Teamwork
- Inspirational leadership

Many fields incorporate these qualities that cannot effectively be duplicated by artificial intelligence or a robot. In fact, I feel with an aging population, these skills will be in greater demand throughout our lifetime. It is common for the "old" to be now caring for the "very old." At the prime of life when most should be freed up to travel and spend inheritance, the need for caregiving and coordination of care for loved ones escalates.

This step shines a spotlight on what feels most *natural* and the areas where we gravitate. The list's spectrum may include graphic design, mechanical ability, music, counseling, painting, teaching, or other skills. Once again, the list of possibilities is extensive.

On my own chart, after identifying my love to create content in my first column, I didn't limit my list in the second column to producing and creating multiple albums and musicals. My love to create expanded to constructing marketing materials and graphics that I put out for years along with each new project. Designing and devising marketing materials was the skill I added to my second column.

Viewing the list of our favorite activities and reviewing our skill-sets will make it easier to define our opportunities along with our purpose and mission *(coming in the **third and fourth columns**)*. After we look for common elements or denominators among the first two columns, what can we discern about our competencies as well as skills from these lists?

> *Listing what we love to do and what our skills are makes it easier to define our purpose and mission.*

DEFINE THE ELEMENTS

Looking for commonalities in the items in columns one and two takes time and patience. We cannot rush this process. This is not meant to be difficult or deep, but instead insightful and inspiring! We may be surprised at what we discover about ourselves. This can be perceptive, probing and even confidence building as we pursue future directions.

Just as the main elements in water are hydrogen and oxygen, our interests and accomplishments consist of multiple components. So on a separate page if needed, we can identify one item noted in column one from the list of favorite activities. Next, we can list all the smaller elements related to that particular line item. Chart number two in this book will help you start this process.

Here is an example of one of my items in column one: I love to produce new songs and albums. To expand my list of elements, I added the following about the specific parts of production I enjoy:

- Tweaking a song in the studio, especially the vocals.
- Producing marketing materials.

- Producing a video that accompanies the release of a song or album.
- Successfully releasing a quality product with all pieces moving together.

In my list, notice I didn't include the actual rewriting of the song, which is a creative act. My list shows that I like the production element of the outcome more than the process of actually rewriting the song, though rewriting is important. The marketing with visuals and video is extremely fun for me, as an additional creative element. Thus, I added marketing creatively to the list as an outflow of those projects.

So for each of the top favorite items in column one, we add sub-categories that relate to the activity. With long lists, we can pick two or three favorite items to start. This task shouldn't be overwhelming. It is important to keep it simple; let the imagination flow. Once we expand our items list in column one, we can make a similar list of sub points for column two, related to our current natural skills. We shouldn't discount something because we feel a bit rusty. Taking time off to raise a family or complete another task doesn't decrease the value of our skills. Many times our abilities improve after we come back to them after a break, so we can take heart! Chart number three at the end of this chapter will help you work through your column two elements.

Just as the main elements in water are hydrogen and oxygen, our interests and accomplishments consist of multiple components.

OVERLAPPING SKILLS

As we work through this process, we will invariably find elements that overlap between our "love-to-do" list and our current skills. Some of my overlapping common denominators include production, project completion, graphics creation, and video marketing. For example, my current natural skills include successfully producing projects. I don't just start them; I also finish them. In that respect, my skill includes production along with execution. Similarly, I have helped others produce songs and materials successfully to move them ahead with their projects, working with multiple personalities and levels.

The last part of the previous statement includes the soft skills necessary to successfully complete the task, which is working with multiple personalities and levels. Also, part of every project is production and marketing. I have listed those as skills, along with the ability to craft, complete and market various projects.

When working on our first two columns, breaking down the steps and elements of each list helps us see the patterns in our aptitudes and abilities. In the section for expanded elements, we also should focus on **feelings** associated with various activities or interests. Why did we list a particular item or skill? It is perfectly fine to focus on what gives us joy and excitement. In fact, I encourage you to do so!

Chart number four at the end of this chapter will help to compare and match some of the elements in both column one and two. This is an important exercise so don't skip this step. So much of life is spent on *doing* and not really *feeling* and *thinking*. Even though the process is fairly simple, it's meant to free up insightful thinking and imagination for future possibilities, which is tremendously exciting!

COLUMN THREE: CHANGE

Now here comes the real fun! Remember, we ought to enjoy this process. The third column will include additional dreams and possibilities that can include types of work, places to live, and even lifestyles to seek. Chart number five at the end of this chapter will help spark the imagination for those different areas. Even though we may have our doubts, my job is to help women see where they are and begin to imagine where they can go next.

The problem most face at this point is negative self-talk and resistance to change. In his book ***Immunity to Change,*** Robert Kegan says, "Courage involves the ability to take action and carry on even when we are afraid."²⁷ Before any of us connect the dots of our common denominators and possibilities, we must be willing to change and transform our vision of the future.

Visual media has the power to induce moments of tremendous self-doubt, yet purposeful action has the power to reap monumental consequences. When our pursuits are based on sound assessments, the scale is substantially weighted for success. Though success is not guaranteed, it is much more likely than if we do nothing.

> *When our pursuits are based on sound assessments, the scale is substantially weighted for success.*

In the film ***Darkest Hour*** (2018), the drama shows how Winston Churchill rose against the tide of a dissenting British cabinet. It was the precipice of World War II, and Churchill, sleepless and angst-filled, knew he must act against a seemingly unstoppable Nazi force conquering Western Europe. With his own party plotting against him, he withstood his darkest hour, rallied a nation, and changed the course of world history.

Without Churchill's action, the tyrant dictator Hitler would have moved unchecked across the continent and could have stolen even our freedoms in the United States. In an unforgettable scene, Churchill implemented change that would lead Britain to war with no guarantee of victory. However, to do nothing was certain suicide for both their nation and 300,000 troops stranded on the beaches of Dunkirk.

Churchill quoted George Bernard Shaw (1856-1950): "Those who never change their minds never change anything." The crucial concept here is metamorphosis—shedding the cocoon of comfort and emerging a wing at a time to become a beautiful butterfly. In filling the third column, it is important to let our imaginations soar. We cannot let fear of change or loss keep us from our dreams.

Many women at halftime have squelched their imagination, buried their dreams, and repressed hope of a new and exciting future. To break out of that inhibiting, fixed mindset takes the active decision to change with a growth mindset. Take some time to imagine, to dream and to formulate a picture of your life. Is there a place you've always dreamt of living? Would you like to travel more for pleasure as well as business? What about giving more to a worthy organization you believe in? Give yourself permission to dream! Chart five at the end of this chapter includes space for types of work, places to live and lifestyle and relationships. The purpose is to help explore and ignite creativity for future dreams and aspirations.

Change is shedding the cocoon of comfort and emerging a wing at a time to become a beautiful butterfly.

COLUMN FOUR: PURPOSE

After considering the elements of the first three columns, we focus on our "why" in column four with purpose and mission. Upon listing future possibilities according our loves, our current and past skills and our dreams, it's time to consider why we are really passionate about a certain area. The "why" will give steam to the little engine to say, "I know I can." Those possibilities can move us to the next chapter, which is to develop additional measurable and achievable skills needed for future achievement.

As an illustration, when completing my fourth column and filling out chart number six, I reviewed my "why," or **mission statement.** *Driven by the desire to encourage and effectively equip women for success, we exist to provide women with all the tools, both technical and mental, that they will need to enjoy more success in the second half of their life than they did in their first.* In the boxes I put:

- Encouragement
- Equip women for success in their second half
- Provide technical and mental tools

I then spent time brainstorming my love of production and what is involved. Part of what was noted in my **purpose statement**, or my "what" was production. *Drawing on both years of experience and the successful implementation of a well-developed business plan and guide, we equip women in every area of their lives to experience success in the second half of life.* In the boxes I put: Producing:

- Virtual events
- Online programs
- Podcasts
- Write books
- Live events

Also for column four, I listed what I currently have that I can use to complete all of those projects. That list included popular and well-produced original songs I can include with my events, videos, podcasts and online programs.

CONNECTING THE OPPORTUNITIES

Chart seven at the end of this chapter helps us connect opportunities with passion, experience and mission. On one side of the chart is a place to define overlapping areas of what we love with our skills and purpose. On the other side we define a dream or opportunity that will correspond or build upon what we've defined in the left column.

Reviewing my dreams and opportunity column, I've noted my desire to travel more with my husband as well as create additional quality online programs that are readily accessible around the globe. Every time a person licenses one of my courses or songs, it feels like there's a small army working on my behalf to fulfill my purpose, which is to provide tools and a plan for a successful second half of life. My time is freed up from day-to-day management unless there is a technical issue.

In my first column, I've noted my ability to produce projects successfully and how I love the creative process. To connect dreams and opportunities in the second column with production, I noted my desire to use more multi media tools in my online programs, such as virtual reality. As I learn to use those tools effectively, I will then be able to train others to do the same. That training incorporates a soft skill.

CORE COMMON DENOMINATOR™

Chart eight is the place to put all this together. This is a very important step because the simplicity of the chart helps to project future skills according to the possibilities noted. Developing or building upon current skills and interests can be defined more succinctly for successful outcomes by spending time with this process.

For example: **I LOVE TO** (love to do) *Create content* **WITH** (skill) *tech and media* **FOR** (mission/purpose) *others to gain momentum and success,* **RESULTING IN** (possibility) *a business that focuses on providing successful tools and principles for women at halftime.* To take action and expand my focus of creating content, I will pursue the skill of creating content including virtual reality. This will be discussed more thoroughly in the next chapter on skills.

For travel, booking select engagements where I can include my husband helps me plan some of our travel together. Creating additional targeted online courses and membership sites will create more time, resources and opportunity to spend my days and weeks how I wish.

I never discount what I have already done. Musicians, writers, and producers create popular songs that get nominated for **GRAMMY Awards,** so I fit in that category. Each woman's natural skills, passion, and impact will be different. Some may have incredible organizational skills or the ability to launch events. Creative people need others with administrative skills. That is why I surround myself with those who possess greater organizational abilities!

DON'T DISCOUNT WORK EXPERIENCE

The field of technology is exploding. Since women are underrepresented in technological fields, those areas could bring further possibilities for halftime women. Organizations will look to diversify their job pool, so we should remain open to additional training that will correspond with our skill sets.

Some mistake their core competency for passion. In other words, just because we can do something doesn't mean we are passionate about doing it. The humanitarian Harriet Tubman[28] said, "Every great dream begins with a dreamer. Always remember, you have within you the strength, the patience, and the passion to reach for the stars to change the world."[29] The combination and concentration of core competency, mission, and passion are where we can find success in life-long work. That self-discovery is the first step toward getting un- stuck at halftime.

> *The combination and concentration of core competency, mission, and passion are where we can find success in life-long work.*

I found the four columns exercise very helpful in empowering me to reboot and reinvent my career. It doesn't take a math wizard *(which I'm not!)* to see the basic string of elements that run through what I love and what I desire to do. Finding the common denominator is actually great fun! My personal journey is anything but over. As a lifelong learner, there are always new areas and opportunities that will become available, especially in the area of technology. Many times those areas are revealed and take place while life happens!

Now is the time to stop and fill out the four columns in the Core Common Denominator™ system. The purpose of this process is to reaffirm abilities and skills as well as unlock creativity and future possibilities. Having a simple, yet effective system as the Core Common

Denominator™ adds enjoyment and clarity to options at halftime, all while increasing pleasure and lessening fear.

BUSINESS STRUCTURE

Chart nine is meant to help map out both our business and personal categories, as they are connected in many ways during halftime. The table included is a basic guide to stimulate our thinking of doing business in person and virtually, online. With online programs, one develops the prospect of a global impact without physical travel, although those programs still need managed.

Part of this discovery is defining your ideal work schedule. Many women balance a number of activities in their life and struggle to find and create time for what they truly enjoy. This becomes even more difficult when one is sandwiched between caring for children and parents. However, with foresight and a workable routine, it is possible to create a viable schedule and structure geared for success.

1. CORE COMMON DENOMINATOR™

Refer to these definitions as you fill out each of your columns

Love	Skills	Opportunities	Purpose
Love to Do	**Current Skills/ Experience**	**Dreams and Opportunities**	**Mission and Purpose**
• Make sure some of these are artistic and recreational. • These should unlock the creative, or right side, of your brain. • Make the list extensive.	• These skills and experiences do not have to be recently used skills but things you know you are good at. • Draw from past experiences that may be lying dormant presently. • Include soft skills which can't be duplicated with artificial intelligence or a robot.	• How do you want to spend your day(s)? • If you could do anything you wanted, what would you do? Responses can include anything from donating your time to a worthy organization, starting your own business to helping an organization grow to its potential.	• This is your WHY? • What are you passionate about? What fuels you? How could you employ that passion to assist others and/or society?

2. LOVE TO DO: COLUMN ONE EXPANSION

CORE COMMON DENOMINATOR™

Be creative and use your imagination. Include anything you want!

"Love to Do"
*These activities can be artistic and recreational.
This list will help unlock the right side of your brain!*

Expand each Element
*Identify the specific parts of what you
love to do—**the why and what.***

I love to... (specific parts of why and what about it...)	1.
	2.
	3.
I love to...	1.
	2.
	3.
I love to...	1.
	2.
	3.

3. SKILLS AND EXPERIENCE: COLUMN TWO EXPANSION

CORE COMMON DENOMINATOR™

Be creative and draw from current and past experience.

Current Skills based on Past Experience
Identify not only your best current skills and experience, but skills from your past, even if they have been lying dormant.

Expand Elements of each Skill
*Next, Identify the **specific parts of each skill** or experience listed. Don't exclude **soft skills**!*

Skill (identify specific parts of what is involved in each skill)	1.	
	2.	
	3.	
Skill	1.	
	2.	
	3.	
Skill	1.	
	2.	
	3.	

4. CONNECTING EXPANDED ELEMENTS

CORE COMMON DENOMINATOR™

List the similar connecting elements noted from both the "love to do" and the "skills and experience" exercises.
*Note **the FEELINGS you experience for each element and WHY**.*

Shared Element

It makes me feel...

_____
_____

Shared Element

It makes me feel...

_____
_____

Shared Element

It makes me feel...

_____
_____

Shared Element

It makes me feel...

_____
_____

5. OPPORTUNITIES AND DREAMS: COLUMN THREE EXPANSION

CORE COMMON DENOMINATOR™

This is the place to put down what you've always wanted to do, no matter how large or outrageous!

WORK	LIVE	LIFESTYLE
Type of Work: Incorporate "soft skills" as well as technical skills.	*Places to Live or Travel. Remember, it's possible to work remotely!*	*Lifestyle and Relationships: How do you want to spend your days?*

6. MISSION & PURPOSE: COLUMN FOUR

CORE COMMON DENOMINATOR™

*This is your **WHY**? What are you **passionate about**? What fuels you? What **effect could exercising your passion have on others and/or society**?*

Compose one main mission statement. (your WHY) To help you, list things that you are passionate about in the boxes below:

Mission Statement

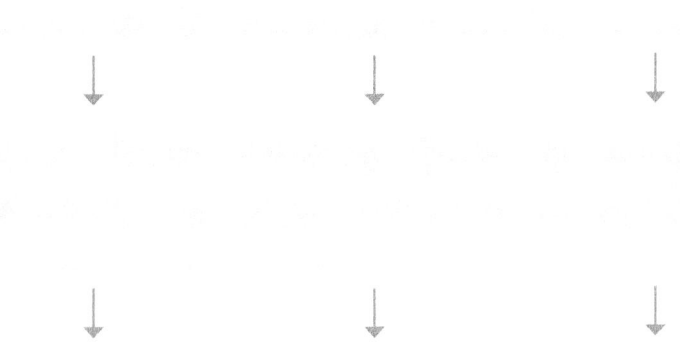

Consider the interests and passions listed above.

What effect will your actions have on others and/or society when you exercise your interests and passions? (your WHAT)

To help you, list actions and interests in the boxes below.

Purpose Statement

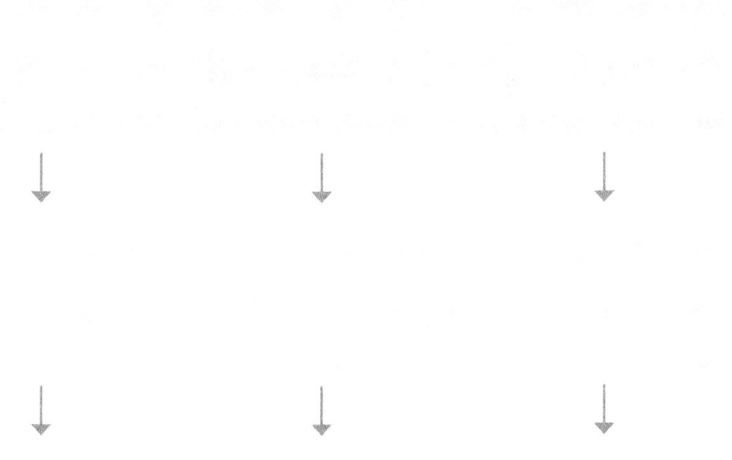

7. CONNECTING THE OPPORTUNITIES

CORE COMMON DENOMINATOR™

Passion + Experience + Mission

LOVE SKILLS PURPOSE	OPPORTUNITIES AND DREAMS
Note some overlapping skills and purpose here from these three columns.	*Incorporate some of the items you noted on your list that would be possible with what you noted to the left.*

8. CORE COMMON DENOMINATOR™

These are some exercises that will help you brainstorm further for solid action.

(love to do) + (skill) + (purpose) = (possibility)

Example: I LOVE TO *Create content* **WITH** *media and tech* **FOR** *others to gain momentum and success,* **RESULTING IN** *a business that focuses on providing successful tools and principles for women at halftime.*

Fill in some of your possibilities:

	1. *(skill)* **with…**
I love to…	2. *(purpose)* **for…**
	3. *(possibility)* **resulting in…**
	1. *(skill)* **with…**
I love to…	2. *(purpose)* **for…**
	3. *(possibility)* **resulting in…**
	1. *(skill)* **with…**
I love to…	2. *(purpose)* **for…**
	3. *(possibility)* **resulting in…**

9. BUSINESS STRUCTURE

*This chart not only includes **business**, but **personal** as they are connected in many ways! You can extend this chart with as many areas and subcategories as you **formatting it to your needs**. Below are "ideas" to get you started. Remember, ONLINE events also have to be **managed** but can free up your time! Keep your **Ideal Work Schedule** in mind.*

A few personal examples:
LIVE Events: *Keynotes-Concerts (per month); Workshops (per month)*
ONLINE Events: *Webinars (per month); Online Summits (per year)*
PERSONAL: *Travel (combined w/business); Family Events*

LIVE Events	ONLINE Events	PERSONAL

10. ACTION ITEMS

IMMEDIATE ACTION ITEMS

1 _____

2 _____

3 _____

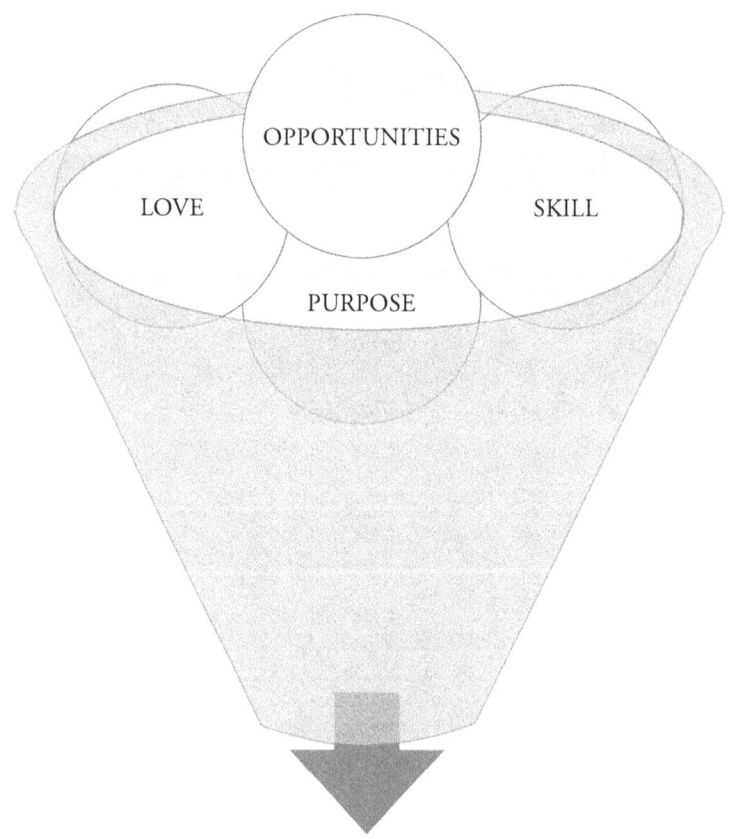

Love**O**pportunity**P**urpose**S**kills
Core Common Denominator™

APPLICATION

Take some time to work and re-work your columns and charts.

1. **Four Columns: Love, Skills, Opportunities, Purpose**

   Refer to definition of all four columns.

2. **Column One: Love**

   Column one based on what you *love to do* and expanded elements.

3. **Column Two: Skills**

   Column two based on *skills and experience* and expanded elements.

4. **Columns One and Two: Love and Skills**

   Column one and two, identifying shared elements and feelings you experience for each element.

5. **Column Three: Opportunities**

   Column three with Dreams and Opportunities, expanded for type of work, places to live, travel, lifestyle and relationships.

6. **Column Four: Purpose**

   Column four with Mission and Purpose expanded with elements of passion and effect on others and/or society.

7. **Connecting Opportunities**

   The first column lists your top combined elements from first three columns, then incorporates some of your dreams and opportunities.

8. **Core Common Denominator™**

   Additional exercises to help you brainstorm further including skill, purpose and possibilities for solid action items.

9. **Business Structure**

   Exercise to define business live and online as well as personal areas, as they are connected in many ways during halftime. This should help define your ideal work schedule.

10. **Action Items**

    Immediate action items including all four columns: Love, Opportunity, Purpose and Skills. (LOPS).

FIVE

Skills Cable

Building skills based upon our competencies is similar to utilizing multiple ropes while climbing. With free solo climbing where no ropes are involved, a climber faces a greater risk of falling. Consequently, most climbers use various aids, like multiple ropes and anchors to get to a mountain summit. These specific ropes are usually 150 to 230 feet in length, so long climbs have to be broken into multiple one hundred to two hundred-foot sections, depending on the rope lengths.

Each anchor driven into the rock will also be a bit different, but should be solid, equalized, redundant, and efficient. So it is in life, those guiding ropes are secured with anchors of competence, commitment, confidence, and tenacity to pursue dreams. Such opportunities become defined goals, helping women develop skills based upon their core competencies to achieve dream objectives. One of my favorite stories of a woman who used her past experience and competence, then built additional skills to scale her Hero Mountain and reinvent herself is that of child actress Shirley Temple, who went on to become a diplomat.

Strong anchors of competence includes commitment,
confidence and tenacity to pursue dreams and opportunities.

Born in 1928, Shirley Temple started her film career at age three. She achieved popular success until her adolescence, when she only appeared in a few films. At twenty-two, she retired from her movie career. Although she performed in some television series and other projects in adulthood, she never found the same success. Her autobiography ***Child Star*** chronicled her journey as that adorable little girl performer Shirley Temple.

I grew up watching Shirley Temple movies. My mother even twirled my waist-length hair into ringlets, so I could emulate Temple's singing and dancing in films like *Bright Eyes, On the Good Ship Lollipop,* and *Curly Top.* Despite her popularity, some critics depicted her as merely raw talent with no formal acting or dance training. In the 1960s, rumors, obviously untrue, spread that she was no child at all but a thirty-year-old dwarf who wore curly wigs. It is interesting that "fake news" proved popular even in that era.

STAR DELEGATE AND NEGOTIATOR

When Shirley Temple's older brother was diagnosed with multiple sclerosis, she joined the ***International Federation of Multiple Sclerosis Society***. Some time later, President Richard M. Nixon appointed Temple as a delegate to the twenty-fourth United Nations General Assembly, which led to her later appointments to diplomatic posts. She proved to be a celebrity appointee who actually did the work of the office. Shirley Temple Black remained interested in international relations and eventually traveled to Czechoslovakia to commemorate their entry into the MS Society.

Temple did her homework as a delegate as she pursued multiple assignments and fervently read books to further her education. She moved beyond the image of Shirley Temple, child star, to earn a reputation as an effective negotiator. Even though her celebrity status opened the doors in these international arenas, it was her diplomatic skills that kept the doors of negotiation open.

Temple served as a diplomat longer than she worked as an actress. Her childhood experiences equipped her to face the challenges in her midlife. She had the skill, sense of humor, perception, intelligence and tenacity to make a great diplomat. According to her daughter Susan, Temple never lost her feminine approach. She would play chess with the representatives from other countries and hold film parties. With confidence and skill, she established relations with both China and the Soviet Union when both countries were hostile toward the U.S.

As a little girl, Temple met many different types of people, so she learned how to make them feel at ease. When she became Chief of Protocol in 1976 at age 48 *(the first female to hold this position)*, she led more than three-dozen staff people who were responsible to teach new ambassadors and their spouses the customs of various countries and political groups. Her natural acting skills became a strength as she performed these tasks!

Shirley Temple Black died February 10, 2014, at 85. She not only had natural talent, but also, she utilized these competencies to serve in government positions and to promote a cure for MS, a disease that affects up to 2.5 million people worldwide. Her achievements can be an example to other women looking to contribute to society in all stages of their lives.

While few of us have ever been child stars, still we have natural skills we can build upon just as Shirley Temple did. In the previous chapter, we constructed charts to discover our core competencies and strengths. Now is a good time to examine our own competency banks. With longer lifespans and advances in technology, it has become more necessary than ever to forge ahead with the willingness to grow, change and risk to face life's second half.[30]

> *While few of us have ever been child stars, still*
> *we have natural skills we can build upon.*

YOUR COMPETENCY BANK

As a little girl, I remember entering the large doors of our local bank with my grandmother. For several years she gave my sisters and I $100 savings bonds, which felt like a million dollars at the time. Even though those bonds didn't amount to a great sum of money, we learned the fundamentals of saving as an important life principle.

Just as a woman maintains a bank account or system of saving and investing, it's important also for her to cultivate, then build upon, her core competencies and strengths. Several roadblocks many women face at halftime include feeling irrelevant, being left behind in a fast-paced workplace, finding themselves unable to learn a new skill, and being seen as technically challenged.

However, the good news is that we can not only dispel those myths but blow them up. First of all, our experience and skills form a solid foundation in our competency bank that will continue to serve us well. Our society and the marketplace are changing, but it is the kind of change that every generation faces.

> *Just as a woman maintains a bank account or system of saving and investing, it's also important for her to cultivate, then build upon, her core competencies and strengths.*

We cannot dismiss the challenges, for change is inevitable, as seen in the way businesses appear or disappear over time. For example, some business franchises popular in 1993 are now extinct, including computer training centers *(now offered online and on YouTube)*, mobile carpet stores, video learning centers *(now available online)*, glamour photography *(use your cellphone!)*, and videocassette rentals. *(Remember the slow death of Blockbuster?)*

Yet good news remains. Many business ventures exist today that didn't in 1993, like property management, physical therapy, lash and brow services, massage and spa centers *(with monthly memberships)*, and paint-and-sip studios. In fact, *Entrepreneur Magazine* received 1,023 applications from companies hoping to get their franchises on the top 500 list. *Entrepreneur's* research shows the service industry is strong with a 5.6 percent increase from mid-2016 to mid-2017.[31] A leading study of over 371 global employers, representing more than thirteen million employees, found that social skills, such as persuasion, emotional intelligence, and teaching, will be in higher demand across industries than the demand for narrow technical skills.[32]

CRYSTALLIZED INTELLIGENCE

Crystallized intelligence is known as the accumulation of facts and knowledge. With research gathered from nearly 50,000 subjects by Joshua K. Hartshorne and Laura T. Germine of Harvard and MIT,[33] the peak for the ability to evaluate other people's emotional states occurred in the late 40's or 50's. Data showed the largest accumulation occurring in the late 60's or early 70's. Researchers believe this may be a result of better education, more reading and more opportunities for intellectual stimulation for older people.[34]

So what does this mean for women like us? To survive, we must identify those firm foundations that can lead us to new options and opportunities. Business areas like food, childcare, recreation and health care all include basic foundations that have essentially remained the same. However, each has evolved to remain relevant. Similarly, if we have a solid base or foundation in our competency banks, we can build upon it to add uniqueness and relevancy to our personal brands and skillsets. The challenge lies in connecting our competence with our passion, then building on our skillset to grow.

In the *Future of Jobs and Skills* study,[35] about two thirds of all industries reported their intentions to invest in the reskilling of employees as part of their change management efforts. These companies are also more than twice as likely to target female talent and minority talent. Further, many older employees remain underutilized, but the hope is that across most industries, employers will make better use of the accumulated experience of mature, seasoned employees to build an ageless workforce. The potential is there if women pursue and create opportunities.

IT STARTS WITH ATTITUDE

Most jobs are reimagined over time. To survive in this new world depends on one's understanding of how the work world functions.[36] Even McDonalds, started in 1955, *(a baby-boomer year!)*, experienced an identity crisis. In recent years, they lost market share and popularity when other fast food businesses offered healthier meal options like hormone-free foods with nicer seating and store interiors. However, McDonalds came back strong to be the number one franchise on *Entrepreneur's* 2017 list.[37]

> *Re-evaluation is often necessary and fruitful for moving forward in a business or one's personal life.*

How does McDonalds' success relate to us? First of all, the company focused on their customers, who loved breakfast and discounts. Their main customer base wasn't looking for organic or gluten free. So they focused first on the food basics their customers preferred.

NOTHING BUT NET

The term **nothing but net**, in basketball lingo, relates to the swishing sound the ball makes when entering the hoop without touching the rim or backboard. It requires an exact aim. In the same way, an exact focus on one's basic skills is conducive to finding the common denominator linking competency and experience. In the arts, that principle of centrality applies extensively to music composing and comedy writing. Crafting a simple, central hook is key to a pop song's success. Similarly, converging on a single idea is crucial to making comedy laugh-out-loud funny.

One of the essential principles of improvisation in comedy is repeating a single idea three times. The three-part repetition forms the basis for the joke's success. An example is to mention something ordinary, then mention something else ordinary. The third time, the comic mentions something ridiculous. Such as, "I go to Las Vegas to see the shows, eat at the buffets and visit my money."[38] It is an unexpected twist on the ordinary. This repetition principle applies to categories, traits, rhymes, places, and many other patterns.

Competency as the central idea is key. Our basic skills are part of our personal bank. We already have an account! It is important to brainstorm every avenue where a competency can take us. As we review our column of dreams and opportunities, it is important to list every job that relates to our various skill sets. In this step, our goal is to expand the list of specific options and possibilities.

> *The faster and busier life gets, the more we need to build thinking and quiet reflection time into our schedules.*

It is vital to spend a good amount of time on this activity. Our fast-paced society stresses immediacy and urgency. Busyness becomes our god and unless every moment is filled, we feel unfulfilled.

In contrast, successful business people take time for reflection. Take billionaire Warren Buffet as an illustration. By his own estimate, Buffet has spent 80 percent of his career reading and thinking. Similarly, the faster and busier life gets, the more we need to build thinking and quiet reflection time into our schedules. There are circumstances in life where down times are provided in an unexpected way. I recently had a colleague share that she was in a *funk*, having just lost one of her top clients, yet she remained determined to claw her way out.

IN A FUNK

I remarked to my friend that being in a funk is not always bad. In fact, a discouraged, funky mood can spark new motivation. However, one has to decide to act. If a woman remains despondent, she could easily develop a victim attitude or sink into despondency. Losing a major client during halftime can bring rediscovery, focus, and empowerment to move us on to new heights. Times of thought and reflection often bring baby steps and then leaps forward, taking us out of dark rooms of panic and fear to a place of renewed goals and strategies.

> *A discouraged, funky mood can spark new motivation.*
> *However, one has to decide to act.*

The world is changing, but there are many aspects of business that have stayed the same, such as good service and quality products. When considering which direction to turn or build upon, I'd like to encourage women to explore additional options in technology because females in tech fields are underrepresented so pursuing that direction may open unexpected doors.

In considering technology, I'm not speaking of learning to code or creating elaborate web designs. There is a form of technology that runs through most fields. For example, some cutting edge hair salons *(no pun intended!)* use apps allowing customers to check in and calculate wait times for appointments. Wouldn't it be wonderful for doctor's offices to do the same? *(Do I hear a loud Amen?)* We don't have to create these apps, but we can become familiar with the technologies that would partner well with business.

Shirley Temple Black set the pace in not only repurposing her previous experience, but also reinventing her life. To prepare for her positions as diplomat and delegate, she poured in the time and energy to read, study, and complete assignments. She was accustomed to long hours, from her work as an actress. Black realized there was no substitute for work, following examples of other leaders, including presidents, entrepreneurs and CEOs of large corporations. In the same way, moving ahead may require long hours of research and preparation to realize our passions in some tangible work.

Yet working hard doesn't necessarily mean working every minute. Remember, we can decide when and how much we want to work. Additionally, if a woman is successful in her current field, she can still expand and grow in that arena. Personal and professional growth fuels excitement and builds momentum, keeping our minds sharp and creative.

> *Working hard doesn't necessarily mean working every minute.*

EXPANDING A BUSINESS

When expanding my business, I increased my platform by creating online learning programs, which presented a technical challenge. Furthermore, after creating my first large video course, I faced a debilitating website hack. *(That became the reason why I wrote the book* ***Bad Code!****)* This problem required that I take all my online programs off my own platform to launch them on an outside learning management system. By doing so, I gained peace of mind and garnered nice reviews. However, my profit and limited control proved problematic and undesirable.

Subsequently, after research and deliberation, I migrated five of my websites, changed my weekly newsletter platform and re-launched the same membership platform I had used previously. Creating individual pages for the instruction and membership took countless hours because I had to re-learn the platform and construct the pages. Even though the process proved frustrating at times, I kept my eyes on the future potential.

When I completed the re-launch, I knew all the hard work would pay off. My work allowed me to promote my own brand instead of another learning platform and to integrate my courses with my other programs. Also, I could further automate my online courses to allow for greater development. Another of my goals was to make sure all online courses looked professional on mobile sites. Purchasing an additional program that worked with *WordPress* accomplished this goal.

My experience shows that we don't need to fear that huge tech wall looming before us. We can find assistance. I hired experts to assist me in my re-launch and took the deep dive to learn. Much help is available, especially online and with video conferencing. In fact, instruction on most any subject with varying expertise is available on YouTube. However, it is always best to seek professional help if needed since we usually get what we pay for.

> *Seek professional help often if needed*
> *since we usually get what we pay for.*

The point is that while learning a new skill, technological or professional, it may take ten times longer to accomplish one small project. So we will need patience in the process! I definitely needed patience when building my music studio and creating large musical scores for publication. Keeping goals and future possibilities in sight is critical.

I constantly hear the following negative statements when discussing new technological skills:

- I am not tech savvy.
- I can't do anything with a computer.
- Computer work is too frustrating.

These barriers need not be a major roadblock. A good manager can learn enough to be able to work effectively even with frustration. If we learn enough in the tech area to manage work, then we can hire out specific jobs reasonably and effectively. The process is not terribly difficult. Even code, in its basic form, is simple. Take the example of binary code.

PRINCIPLE OF BINARY CODE RELATING TO TECHNOLOGY

Binary code consists of the numbers 0 and 1, repeated in different combinations. To look at a long string of numbers can cause our eyes to cross. But if we break it down to groups of two, it's like basic addition. What's 2+2? Four! Now add another number to the mix. 2+2+3. It's seven! Let's do one more. 2+2+3+7. Fourteen!

If we consider a longer example, we may panic at the sight of 2+2+3+7+1+8+9+3+5+4+9. Yikes! We want to run for our calculators! There's no way someone can figure that sum out in seconds unless she has a mathematical mind like my husband. However, if we organize the numbers into groups of two, just like our beginning math problem, the computation is manageable: (2+2)=4, (3+7)=10. Together, that's fourteen. Then we add (1+8)=23 and so on. Thus, when we break the addition down to groups of two, it's much easier to solve the problem accurately and quickly.

Technology works in much the same way. If we discover the basics, then we can understand, build upon, and implement code. For example, I just purchased a compact projector for presentations given in small rooms. However, when I tried to use it, *(The night before a presentation of course!)*, the image was reversed and upside-down. The projector manual included tiny print in four languages indecipherable even with a magnifying glass. Next, I looked online for guidelines or forums with no success. Rebooting the projector didn't work either. Before giving up and sending the machine back to Amazon, I started pressing buttons on the remote.

There had to be a simple solution since the device had great reviews. As I continued my sequence of button-pushing, Eureka! I solved the problem with the push of two basic buttons. It seemed so simple after that. I noted the simple commands and attached the instructions to the projector. What seemed like a major challenge was solved by two simple commands in the correct order.

That experience gave me confidence to face the next tech challenge. Mastering technology is not an unreachable prospect. If we can control our frustration, we can solve inscrutable problems. We just can't quit too soon!

> *Whatever the area of your focus, many times the tech principles will be simple and easy to implement; however, you can't give up too soon!*

BUILDING SKILLS

Malcom Gladwell, in his book ***Outliers***[39], speaks of the 10,000-hour rule. His research shows that by putting in ten thousand hours performing a task, a person can develop a new skill. However, this statistic is misleading because in mastering an instrument, 10,000 hours of practice is just a start.

Proficiency and progress require many more hours of learning new works, improving technique, and keeping skills sharp. It also takes specific, perfect practice. Such proficiency requires an attitude of lifelong learning. At halftime, most women don't have or desire to spend 10,000 hours to develop a new skill. So it is important to identify where we want to put our time and what we would like to develop.

In *Essentialism*, Greg McKeown garnered data from over five hundred individuals about their experience of learning a new skill as a part of more than one thousand teams. The studies showed that lack of clarity brought confusion, stress, frustration and ultimately failure. The prognosis? Clarity equals success.[40] Clearly defining our goals, specifically focusing on our uniqueness and passion, will help us develop the right skill. There are no guarantees of complete success, but we will definitely increase our chances.

In today's clone society, it is important to set ourselves apart. Distinctiveness can jet-propel our plans. Cal Newport in *So Good*

They Can't Ignore You explains the craftsman mindset: *It asks you to leave behind self-centered concerns about whether your job is 'just right,' and instead put your head down and plug away at getting really damn good. No one owes you a great career; you need to earn it and the process won't be easy.*[41]

> *In today's society of clones, it is more important than ever to set ourselves apart with distinctiveness to jet-propel our plans.*

DEFINE AND DECIDE

It is defeating to think about age and how the years are ticking by. Focusing on fatigue or lack of sleep can also make a woman feel discouraged. Such foci are time wasters. Instead we first define, then initiate an action plan to build on present or dormant skills. Just as building blocks are stacked on top of a firm base, we need time to define our base.

Discomfort in our present position can indicate the need for change. Halftime is the perfect place to make that change. A woman's experience, skill, freedom of time and even financial flexibility are all advantages. It's entirely possible for her to keep working into her seventies and even eighties.

> *If we're not comfortable in our present position, it is a good indicator that we need change.*

The time we spend now defining our second half will have benefits both personally and professionally. Developing skills doesn't mean being perfect. Instead we embrace self-improvement and fulfillment but avoid perfectionism with its unachievable goals.

Most of us are not child stars with opportunities like Shirley Temple's. Yet even Temple didn't depend on her early success for her adult career track. The world is full of *has-beens* who tout only former achievements. I have seen many "stuck" performers whose past successes are not enough to secure them ongoing opportunities. For example, some sopranos depend on their experience playing the role of Christine in a *Phantom of the Opera* production to qualify them for other engagements. However, they sing with a vibrato wide enough to drive a truck through, seemingly unaware that such a singing style limits their chance for future employment. Like many former one-hit wonders who topped the Billboard charts, it is difficult to keep such limited career options alive.

Past accomplishments, no matter how grand, do not guarantee future success although they do provide an anchor to build upon. Consistent healthy habits, connection with an audience, and an authentic message are characteristics that carry a performing career through the decades, leading her to the top of Hero Mountain.

The great pianist Roger Williams, as he continued performing, consistently practiced descending chromatic thirds, a musical motif that propelled his arrangement of **"Autumn Leaves"** to Billboard success in 1955. Because of his commitment to his craft, he performed well into his eighties until pancreatic cancer took his life.

> *Past accomplishments, no matter how grand,*
> *do not guarantee future success, although*
> *they do provide an anchor to build upon.*

Tony Bennett, another exemplary entertainer, still performs at ninety-one years young. I heard him sing at the Hollywood Bowl when he turned eighty and stood amazed at his vocal chops then, as he hit even the high notes. This eighteen-time GRAMMY Award Winner knew how to reinvent his life, as he has developed the discipline of healthy vocal habits to keep performing at a top level. His good routines forged a healthy path to guide him through his long career. A good path, as opposed to a bad rut, is a management tool that has kept Bennett doing what he loves, being a legendary crooner. Additionally, Bennett's strong anchors of talent and vocal health have brought him opportunities to record with Lady Gaga, Elton John, Michael Bublé, Andrea Bocelli, Diana Krall, Stevie Wonder, B.B. King, and Billy Joel among others.

To continue pursuing the column of dreams and opportunities, remember that the demand across industries will still be those social skills of persuasion, emotional intelligence and teaching others. If any of those are in our competency bank, they are strong anchors to hold cables that are solid, equalized, redundant, and efficient with a scope limited to our uniqueness.

The expansion of skills, built upon a competency bank account of strengths, will infuse confidence and commitment for advancement. Our summit of dreams and opportunity suddenly becomes clearer and obtainable when our goals are clearly in sight!

HARD AND SOFT SKILLS

Women who feel insignificant and irrelevant at halftime should understand how valuable their life skills, including soft skills, are. Even if entering a field using additional technology, the demand for those who can effectively work with people will never diminish and will probably grow in the future. Soft skills are transferrable across many fields and should be listed in one's competency bank.

US News posted the 100 best jobs, and some are listed below to spark the imagination.[42] Notice that many are in the medical field and most fields are multi-generational in scope. Don't leave an area out that sparks your imagination solely because of a fear of technical abilities. Remember the main four domains of soft skills: self-awareness, self-management, social awareness and relational management. Within those four domains are twelve emotional intelligence competencies of which many can be applied to most any field in some way. The brain may be slower than a computer, but it's smart enough to build a computer. A computer can't build a brain!

Software Developer	Nurse Anesthetist
Dentist	Optometrist
Physician Assistant	Actuary
Nurse Practitioner	Mathematician
Orthodontist	Diagnostic Medical Sonographer
Statistician	Cost Estimator
Pediatrician	Business Operations Manager
Obstetrician and Gynecologist	Podiatrist
Oral and Maxillofacial Surgeon	Veterinarian
Physician	Radiation Therapist
Occupational Therapist	Information Security Analyst
Physical Therapist	Lawyer
Anesthesiologist	Mechanical Engineer
Surgeon	Nurse Midwife
Psychiatrist	Accountant
Prosthodontics	Financial Advisor
Dental Hygienist	Speech-Language Pathologist Civil Engineer
Registered Nurse	Financial Manager
Marketing Manager	IT Manager
Physical Therapist Assistant	Massage Therapist
Respiratory Therapist	

FOR THOSE WHO WANT TO ADVANCE

It is important at this point, to return to exercises with the four-column chart in the previous chapter. In the chart's expansion of four columns, we defined what we would like to do, taking into account our common denominators of skill, passion and mission. Hopefully we spent a little time dreaming. The challenge at midlife comes when women must decide whether to remain static, retreat, or advance.

This book is for those who want to advance. The cables of success needed as one climbs Hero Mountain require an attitude of effort and work. Re-evaluation is often necessary and fruitful for moving forward in a business or one's personal life.

Don't rush this process. The tendency is to fill in the blanks and make quick decisions. Remember the words of our sixteenth president Abraham Lincoln, "Give me six hours to chop down a tree and I will spend the first four sharpening the axe." Spend plenty of time thinking and planning. Once a competency bank is defined and new skills are determined, there is an increased chance of success with systematic habits based upon a plan and strategy.

Evaluating Lincoln's quote, he spent two-thirds of his time planning. Warren Buffett spent 80% of his time reading and thinking. In comparison, the result of spending a couple extra weeks or months reviewing this process defining your competency and strategy for developing skills may prove extremely valuable.

1. SKILL EXPANSION

SKILL

List a skill from your second column or a new skill you'd like to develop. It can be a hard or soft skill.

REIMAGINED

Think of way(s) you can use this skill, possibly in a new field or with a new focus.

EXPANDED

What sort of training or program will help you develop this skill further?

Skills	• Reimagined • Expanded
Skills	• Reimagined • Expanded
Skills	• Reimagined • Expanded
Skills	• Reimagined • Expanded
Skills	• Reimagined • Expanded
Skills	• Reimagined • Expanded

2. SKILL TIMELINE

Skill One	Month One Goal:	
	Completed:	
	Month Two Goal:	
	Completed:	
	Month Three Goal:	
	Completed:	
Skill Two	Month One Goal:	
	Completed:	
	Month Two Goal:	
	Completed:	
	Month Three Goal:	
	Completed:	

APPLICATION

Evaluate what's in your Competency Bank. Don't discount your past experience, especially social and soft skills, and interacting effectively with others.

_____

_____

In what ways can you reimagine your future based on your skill set along with your present or past jobs?

_____

_____

Estimate how much time you spend reading and reflecting. Set a weekly goal and write it here.

_____

_____

Write down two defined goals that incorporate at least one of your listed items in your dreams and opportunities column.

_____

_____

How can technology help you further your life or goals in business?

_____

_____

What will be your next step in using or learning more technology?

_____

_____

Spend some time expanding your columns further with additional dreams and opportunities. Don't limit yourself—it's okay to take some risks!

_____

_____

> *Part of the agenda for the Hero Mountain® live Summit for Women at Halftime is taking the time to think about you, your skills and where you are headed in your second half. We partner with you and your story to create focus, momentum and success. Take that time for yourself. You are worth it!*

SIX

HABITS CABLE

Training for mountain climbing is no different than preparing for other fields. It's important to start with a plan. Many factors can get in the way of actually starting, like demands of a current job, commitment to family, or lack of motivation, but creating a plan with the end in mind helps one to put a reasonable training program in place.

Just as mountain climbers complete their ascents in stages, depending on the lengths of their ropes, mid-life professionals can move forward a step at a time to realize short-term goals. Each woman will have different levels, speed, or abilities. The principle gained from the climbing ropes is directly applicable to any lifetime or professional goal. It is possible to achieve success, one rope at a time. Putting off this step will only delay the satisfaction and excitement of moving toward the summit.

Most professional athletes visualize the end goal, winning the competition. Michael Phelps, Olympic swimmer with twenty-eight medals, is one of the most decorated Olympians in history. In an interview with CNBC, he related **five powerhouse habits** he rigorously followed. His ideas illustrate a successful journey for those pursuing career change.

Phelps' first habit is to **write down goals** and keep them on his nightstand, both long-term and short-term goals. He realizes when he puts his goals and dreams on paper, there is *usually an extra step* of commitment and obligation in fulfilling those goals.

His second habit is **never to use the word** *can't*. Taking *can't* out of his vocabulary eliminates a defeatist attitude, which is the opposite of a winning attitude. In the same way, a dynamic mindset requires one to *be prepared to adjust, move, and change* with an "I can" mindset.

Phelps' third habit is his willingness to **give up a lot.** Swimming seven days a week and staying in optimal physical shape doesn't leave much time for other activities. Along with keeping fit, he sleeps a lot, especially when training. He knows that by getting rest, he gives his body and brain time to renew itself. Emotional as well as physical refreshment help him perform at an optimal level.

The fourth habit is to **use other people's trash talk as fuel.** This same strategy applies to our own self-induced head trash talk and also pushes us to face others who may ridicule our personal habits or goals. Michael used those intimidating comments, his competitor's trash talk, for his motivation to *push and compete harder.*

Phelps' fifth habit is to **stay in his lane**, similar to driving in our own traffic lane. Every day, hour, and moment bring a myriad of distractions. Phelps comments on his focus: "I can't control what other people do, so for me, I was always worried about myself and worried about what I needed to do. And, it worked."[43]

Staying on track with a winning and successful idea, sticking with it and remaining in our lane will bring higher and more successful results.

BREAKING OUT OF NEGATIVE RUTS

Halftime is a great season to break out of negative ruts and endless pursuits to nowhere by developing some short-term goals. For example, I defined my ideal work schedule as working from a home office with flexible hours; most days I start early. One of my goals is to do projects that create residual income. In essence, such projects keep working for me long after I complete the project. I also desire to do leisure travel with my husband rather than travel for solo work. So I am choosing to create online programs that are accessible worldwide. Further, I am willing to work many hours as I love what I do, especially as I can take breaks when I desire.

Steven Pressfield in *The War of Art* says, "Procrastination is the most common manifestation of resistance because it's the easiest to rationalize."[44] The Hero Mountain® summit includes dreams realized and opportunities fulfilled based on anchors of competency, but as previously mentioned, we must *start!* Knowledge, skills, and passion can work simultaneously to stimulate a woman's master plan at halftime when that plan is put in place. In developing new habits, we define not only the summit, but a blueprint that includes an ideal schedule to get us there.

A defined schedule and strategy are valuable as they both act as self-management and planning tools. To begin, we must ask ourselves these questions:

- How much time do I want to spend working?
- For what type of organization or business do I want to work?
- How much do I want to travel for work?

Many experts like Timothy Ferriss have modeled the planning process. In his book, ***The 4-Hour Workweek***,[45] he defined his plan in this way: *A desire for a mobile lifestyle and freedom of time and place in his life.* To complete his plan, Ferriss created systems for his own *expert* status and accomplished his goal even while working 14-hour days at another company. Ferriss achieved success and staying power with his plan.

The important point here is not only to define the dream, but also devise an ideal work schedule that produces a satisfactory lifestyle.

All of this can be done while still climbing, using cables of healthy habits to reach the summit. It's not necessary to work 60-80 hours per week at halftime!

THE SEARCH FOR EXPERTS

A Google search for the term "expert" turns up over 370 million results. Today, so-called *experts* sprout up every week. Myriad blogs and articles explain how to become an *expert*. However, to become truly *expert* requires quality training and strong, focused habits.

For instance, consider figure skater Scott Hamilton, a 1984 Olympic Gold Medalist, who learned through endless failure. His habit included starting at 6:45 A.M. to master tracing figure eights on the ice. He confessed, *I was terrible!* However, he had already persevered through a mysterious illness that stunted his growth, so he was not a quitter. His skating career, begun at age nine, actually improved his health. Still it took years before his skill mirrored his drive.

Further, consider Steve Spangler, an Emmy Award winning scientist, who based his *Spangler Effect* on repetition. He had interest in science and started by giving speeches in school assemblies, 4,500 of them. Next, he hosted a kid's weekly science show on NBC. After 240 segments and an Emmy, he then produced over 1,400 segments as the science guy on Denver, Colorado's NBC affiliate. From there, he branched out to large corporate events.[46]

The resiliency already created in life will propel us toward creating new habits and skills.

Thus, Steve used a scientific approach to find and meet a need. After viewing Steve's performance at the National Speaker's Conference, in 2016. I was not only amazed by the amount of smoke and colorful explosions he produced on the stage but also by his humor and confidence before a discerning audience of his peers! With precise timing and skill, he executed what appeared unthinkable on stage. Definitely, Steve is an *expert*.

At this point, we may be thinking,

- I don't have the kind of time at this point in my life to do all those repetitions.
- It's too late for me; I'm not nine years old or even thirty years old!
- I'm too tired to begin something new.
- I don't want to work that hard!

It is never too late. We can be encouraged by recognizing the many repetitions we have already tackled. We have conquered unique challenges by falling down and getting up, numerous times. That resiliency, already created, can propel us toward creating new habits and skills. We can be inspired by Scott Hamilton's clear message. Even though he fell down 41,600 times in his career, he got up 41,600 times. Let's not quit; there is more for us to do.

DANGER OF CHEAP AMBITION

Lose weight now! Become an expert in four weeks! Earn thousands every month! A new slogan has been added to these common get-rich-quick pitches: "Become an Expert in four easy steps!" These thrifty shortcuts fuel a cheap ambition that lacks a solid foundation. Whether a woman at mid-life is starting a new business, joining the board of a non-profit organization, or leading a women's church group, her mindset is important. She must recognize and value her expertise. Her individual proficiencies and sense of confidence and worth form a strong foundation on which she can build further accomplishments.

For example, I developed my piano performance skills through many years of early practice sessions, playing rote scales and drills, and then memorizing thousands of musical scores. While I had innate ability that allowed me to hear and then play a musical line, I also invested in quality coaching and musical instruction. It was necessary for me to develop that skill with a focused mindset.

It's ridiculous to think I could have become a concert pianist merely by sheer talent alone. My achievement required hard work, discipline, dedication, and training. Motivational speakers can pump up audiences with positive principles on becoming proficient and successful in a new field. Yet without quality training and the development of critical habits, such achievement is impossible.

Sales is a skill most every person and organization need to develop, whether as a volunteer or for-profit business. We must be sold on our own capabilities first.

The idea of early and easy success is an assumption often made by those in multi-level organizations where new members are struggling to sell product and develop their down-line. Making sales is a skill every person and organization needs to develop, whether as a charity volunteer or an employee working for a profitable business. We must be sold on our own capabilities first. However, emphasis on positive thinking is not enough.

Furthermore, we must not compare our experience to our colleagues. Nor should we discount our own aptitudes and abilities. We can develop our present skills into valuable assets by honing the right habits. Our proficiency and education make us unique and can define our individual plans. The time we have already spent on our careers, volunteering or raising our families has not been wasted but has value!

We must decide to move our lives forward, to learn or develop skills or build on our life's purpose. There are very few quick fixes in life, but at halftime, reinventing and rebuilding a life takes much less time because of our experience and knowledge.

However, a successful plan requires much thought, a realistic strategy, and achievable goals. It is dangerous to pursue quick answers that create a *cheap ambition*. Good plans have staying power while hasty solutions are built upon shifting sand.

NECESSARY AMBITION

The contrast to cheap ambition is necessary ambition. Climbing our own Hero Mountain successfully comes with a cost of determination, consistency and strong, intentional routines. *Get in shape now! Set new goals to lose weight!* Those phrases appeal to the emotions. Most want to feel good, be in shape, and lose some weight. However, if basic behaviors and mindsets are not confronted with productive changes, the yo-yo effect will become a lifestyle. For this reason, after losing weight, most people gain all the pounds back and more. Every year, gyms make money with new signups, overselling memberships based on escalating drop-off rates.

Yet we don't have to be stuck in an endless yo-yo cycle if we make slight changes in our belief systems. It's not about a resolution, program, diet, or regimen. It is a principle that says, *If I develop productive routines, then apply disciplined consistency to those routines, positive change will happen.* That new regularity transforms into good habits. Discovering how to develop those habits will bring freedom and change in our thoughts and feelings.

Good habits help us apply the principles of discipline into our lives. This growth process is about us, not about those around us, whether it be spouses, children, or coworkers. When we successfully experience change, others will notice and will want to join in the experience. Change requires commitment of time and effort, but those actions bring hope. Making real, positive change reassures us that our efforts are not futile or ineffective.

Consistency and a strong routine are keys to success during halftime years and beyond. Necessary ambition is not cheap but is within reach. Acquiring and building core habits is essential for each woman, but the move doesn't mean giving up chocolate, wine, or pasta. *(I'm definitely not giving up any of those!)* However, it does mean paying attention to schedules, sleep, nutrition, exercise, personal and professional relationships, and one's spiritual life.

> *Necessary ambition is not cheap
> but isn't out of reach either.*

Many people cling to destructive or lazy habits, sabotaging the very changes they envision. Such resistance is like driving a car with one foot on the gas and the other on the brake. We are *thinking* about change while *keeping* life the same. That divided approach results in a jerky ride[47] that burns energy with little progress.

In recent years, the term *positive thinking* has been overused as a replacement for ambition and skill. I am all for *thinking positively* but *thinking* alone cannot accomplish authentic change. Further, repeating positive phrases to ourselves is no guarantee of life change. Good intentions alone form the flimsy foundation of trite thinking. Like putting a band-aid on a hemorrhaging wound, it won't stop the bleeding.

Change comes when we apply the principle of a strong, healthy routine with consistency. Change is the fertilizer of hope, and hope is the fuel of positivity. This endeavor must be founded upon an accurate assessment of our individuality.

> *Change is the fertilizer of hope
> and hope is the fuel of positivity.*

For example, God gave me a natural ear for music. Yet my ambition required my commitment to develop my craft. It meant hours of drills and expanding my repertoire to further my natural skill. In retrospect, it took both a technical and adaptive approach to create the habits necessary to reach my goals.

TECHNICAL VERSUS ADAPTIVE APPROACHES

Defining and then simplifying both the technical and adaptive approaches create habits that bring true change. This concept does not result from deep, subjective data but stems from an important psychological principle. A technical approach is *doing* versus *not doing*, like deciding not to eat food versus eating different foods or exercising versus not exercising or asking more questions versus responding in haste.

Technical Approach

A technical approach incorporates good systems that include cues and rewards. In **The Power of Habit**, Charles Duhigg writes, "A cue is a trigger that tells your brain to go into automatic mode and which habit to use." In theatre or in a musical performance, a *performer's cue* is something a prompter says that signals the onset of speaking, playing or action. The reward is recalling the line or habit correctly.

We respond to cues because our brain has figured out the routine is worth remembering and following for future reward.[48] However, true transformation doesn't end merely with rote adjustments. Creating a legitimate alteration requires a change in lifestyle that incorporates positive mindsets that modify feelings and emotions; that defines an adaptive approach.

> *True transformation doesn't end merely with rote adjustments.*

Adaptive Approach

An adaptive approach includes a shift in belief systems about ourselves; It is not a program we follow but a deep-rooted desire. Those desires can include the aspiration to purchase a new wardrobe that not only fits now, but six months to a year from now. It can include the desire to travel comfortably and not have to wedge tightly into an airline seat, creating an uncomfortable situation. It can also entail the passion to live a healthy life to live long enough to enjoy grandchildren and great grandchildren. All are emotional decisions that take positive action to fulfill.

Take oral health for example. In the early 1900s, toothpaste was not widely used. In fact, the health of American's teeth steeply declined due to the rise of sugary foods. When Claude C. Hopkins, a prominent marketing guru, identified the filmy layer on the teeth as mucin plaque, he focused on the use of toothpaste to eliminate the cloudy film covering teeth. He appealed to consumer desire for good-looking teeth, not dental health. Thus, Hopkins created a *craving for beauty* based on an *emotional response.* Hopkins knew a strong appetite made a cues and rewards system work. Sales skyrocketed, so **Pepsodent** became a household brand that consumers used daily.[49]

Furthermore, training as a concert pianist includes the study of technical scales and drills. I spent daily practice sessions repeating exercises and specific musical passages during early morning hours. As a result, I could master increasingly difficult compositions. However, technique alone doesn't create a quality musician, for technical playing sounds mechanical and machine-like. A true artist builds on good technique to perform a composition that is both beautiful and expressive. My playing had to include both technical skills that came from practice along with an ability to express the beauty or passion of the music.

> *Adaptive change that includes a shift in our own belief system about ourselves affects our whole mindset.*

Focusing only on *dos and don'ts* with diets and workout routines results in dieters regaining weight, rising obesity rates, and declining fitness club attendance. Adaptive change that includes a shift in personal belief systems affects our mindsets. The goal shifts from merely losing weight or getting in shape to committing to a purposeful lifestyle of eating and exercise.

In music, my goal wasn't to master *Hanon* or *Dohnanyi* piano exercises, but to expand my technique in order to play the next large concerto that I loved. The exercises were a means not an end.

That is why, after mastering progressively difficult technical exercises, I ambitiously sought pieces beyond my reach. For example, I was motivated by the challenge of difficult compositions like **Rondo Capriccioso,** by Felix Mendelssohn (1809-1847), which surprised my instructor. I had to improve drastically to master it. However, I did just that! The challenge motivated me.

This approach works well for managers, too. Leaders who merely give more time for questions from their leadership teams can easily apply adaptive change. To do so, the objective is to become attentive and observant, creating a culture of openness and authentic sharing. Establishing honest, clear communication about workers' feelings and beliefs regarding a particular work problem or project will do more to mend relationships than merely focusing on asking questions to get surface feedback.

Leaders who create a culture of openness and authentic sharing with honest and clear communication about feelings and beliefs mend relationships.

IMPORTANT HABITS AT HALFTIME

Each woman must select which habits to establish, revise, or continue. Developing a new routine is a personal decision. No one else can define and establish our habits. Personal adaptive application for life will spring from an emotional desire and commitment.

Important habits at halftime include proper sleep, diet, exercise, financial responsibility, relationship building, spiritual reflection, and knowledge seeking. There are technical aspects of all those basic routines. If procedural principles alone keep us moving ahead, great! What's that old saying? *If it's not broken, don't fix it!* However, the mindset of an adaptive lifestyle will create a greater possibility for lasting and authentic change to move life's football a little closer to the goal line. This section will focus on three categories of habits: Physical, Fiscal and Relational.

Physical: Sleep

First, the basics of physical habits begin with sleep and exercise, which greatly affect focus and fatigue. When a woman's body changes during halftime and menopause arrives, normal routines are disturbed. For some, sleep is often interrupted and irregular. Insomnia, restlessness and exhaustion set in. The old adage of counting sheep becomes almost comical when we're tired and on edge. We feel like kicking those darn sheep across the room!

I have been guilty of skipping precious hours of sleep to finish projects, especially when I am approaching a deadline. Catching up on lost slumber proves difficult for me. My most productive work time is in the early morning hours in contrast to many of my night owl musician-artist friends, who work best during the evening.

Sleep is essential as a renewing treatment for the brain.

There is no right or wrong way in deciding the makeup of a routine, but a consistent schedule that includes sufficient sleep is extremely important. In fact, research confirms that sleep is an essential renewing treatment for the brain. With today's multiple distractions, it is difficult to get the quality rest one needs. Many experts recommend turning off devices up to two hours before retiring. The stimulus from electronic devices delays the body's internal clock, suppressing the release of melatonin. That suppression delays the onset of REM sleep, which should account for at least 20 percent of sleep.[50]

To deal with sleep issues requires us to put a specific plan in place. I have often heard: *I only need a few hours of sleep;* or *My body just doesn't need a lot of sleep.* Yet I guarantee that a lack of sufficient sleep does have a negative impact on our energy levels and concentration. The body as well as the brain needs time to rejuvenate, renew, and rest. In the same way, too much sleep is also unhealthy, so it's important to define individual schedules by focusing on what works best.

Physical: Diet

Chemical imbalances and lack of focus can be directly influenced by diet at halftime. With age, our bodies change. Many notice changes in their chests; they're larger, droopier or smaller. Clothes that once accentuated a well-defined waist don't quite fit the same. That is why we see ads galore about magic foods to eliminate belly fat. While body changes are inescapable, healthy eating and exercise routines can help us maintain energy as well as physique. We can still enjoy many foods, along with the comradeship that happens over food. It's all about choices.

> *Healthy eating and certain exercise routines can help us maintain energy as well as physique. It's all about good choices.*

During a break from work, a task or a meeting, it's normal to grab a snack. Part of that is habitual, but another part is for energy. The fluctuation of blood sugar levels varies from person to person. There are countless books about what to eat, when to eat, and how much to eat for varying glucose levels.

Here, we will talk about habits and how we treat food as a reward. In the brain, dopamine acts as a neurotransmitter to help control the brain's reward and pleasure centers. For example, when I take a break from work, the food I eat acts as a reward that gives me a dopamine rush, telling my body I have renewed energy and focus. Depending on the type of snack I consume, this can be a short-lived boost with a sugar crash, or long-lasting boost fueled by an energy producing protein.

For a similar reward with different, yet sustaining results, we can replace the routine snack with a short hike or walk. Doing activity consistently will create a new, sound habit. This is how habits are replaced by using the trigger and reward system that Duhigg proposes in his book. To carry Duhigg's concept a step further for adaptive change, we can create a mental image of ourselves walking, concentrating on how it makes us feel. *(We focus on the good feelings, not just how tired we are walking up a hill!)* Imagine the boost of energy we will feel after a walk and what we will accomplish afterward.

This repeated behavior of walking during breaks, gives a boost of energy we remember. When we envision the experience to create a mental image of what we need, we are employing adaptive change. It is much more than technical repetition for a number of days. The emotion works to create and cement lasting change. Functioning technically, we would just pass up the donut or sugary snack to eat something else like carrot sticks or celery. But with an adaptive mindset, we are creating a mental image and a new feeling for a lifestyle change that goes beyond losing pounds or lowering blood sugar.

> *Adaptive change is much more than technical repetition for a number of days; it cements an emotion to create lasting change.*

Similarly, it is a good idea to evaluate what we eat consistently. According to a survey taken of 9,248 diners across the U.S., the national average for dining out was 4.5 times per week.[51] It is more difficult to make healthy choices when eating out, but not impossible. An attitude of *healthy lifestyle eating* will help women make healthy decisions. As an illustration, one of our sons, who is an attorney, put on thirty pounds of muscle during college. He has maintained his muscle mass and physique even while working long days. He brings healthy snacks to his office and is regimented in his choices as it helps him retain his energy throughout the day even when working at a sedentary job.

What are those healthy choices and snacks? A heart-healthy Mediterranean diet that includes fruits, vegetables, fish, whole grains and good fats is a good approach. In an age of information access, we can find a diet program that fits any taste. My advice is not to focus on a diet but on a lifestyle.

My personal regimen includes a healthy low-calorie snack every two to three hours. I love fruits and vegetables, but I also love the carbs. If I find my clothes aren't fitting well, I avoid carbs and prepare more salads, piling on the vegetables but using light dressing. I make a choice to eat healthy because I know that it's easier to grab a bag of whole-wheat *healthy* crackers when I'm in a rush. Yet by doing so, I quickly consume over one thousand calories! The secret is finding what works for our body types, but it doesn't mean starving ourselves. Women who need a program to help them should join one of the various eating plans. However, the focus should remain on the *lifestyle* we're creating not just a diet.

Physical: Exercise

There are many documented benefits to exercise, especially at halftime. Just like eating plans, exercise plans are personal. We need to discover and apply what works best for each of us. To stay fit leads to a better quality of life. Especially noteworthy is the reduction of fall-related fractures by 40 percent or more with physical activity.[52] Most surveyed in the 2018 U.S. government health scientific report were age fifty and above, but for those younger than fifty, healthy routines will lead to years of benefits. We may not notice it now, but as our bodies age, muscle strength wanes, so a woman's sense of balance weakens, making her prone to falls and injuries.

> *Even if younger than fifty, healthy routines will lead to years of benefits.*

In fact, I experienced this danger first hand when last year, my husband Greg developed an infection in the bone of his big toe. Now, Greg is six-three with very large toes that take up almost half of his foot. The infection proved so severe that doctors warned he might lose his toe if treatment didn't succeed. Since my husband is also a former professional athlete, the possibility of losing that toe brought him great fear and alarm.

His concern was reflected in many of his comments like, "This may be the last time we get to take a walk like this together." Such statements were common. However, after surgery, surviving a pic line, and keeping the foot elevated for six months by riding a scooter, Greg and his toe recovered. He currently has a clean bill of health. So, we are most grateful. However, an unexpected side benefit arose from that health crisis. Greg received physical therapy that helped his posture, stride, and balance.

I'm mentioning the benefits Greg received because he still worked out like an athlete, yet he was experiencing difficulty with balance, walking flat-footed with his large frame. The physical therapist gave him new exercises that remedied those problems. Even though it was physically difficult at times, his new routine will ensure better health for his next ten to twenty years.

THE YEAR OF THE TOE

Our *Year of the Toe* taught us some good principles for halftime and beyond. What we have always done in the past may need revision for the future. As I observe my aging parents, who no longer dance but now shuffle along with stooped shoulders, it's easy to see how gravity naturally pulls us down.

A fitness program doesn't need to be difficult, but it does require regular time in our weekly regimen. We should include weights and balance exercises as well as cardio. It is not about building huge muscles but building strength and tone. Even brisk walks that get our heart rates up will work as part of our cardio routine. We can double-dip on our time and enjoyment by taking our dogs along!

> *What we have always done in the past*
> *may need revisions for the future.*

In my routine, I send my body to the gym early, almost every morning. My mind usually follows about halfway through my workout, which includes a combination of cycling and weights. One of the considerable benefits, besides the good way I feel afterward, is the mental diversion it creates. Some of the rote exercises allow my mind to think and imagine, especially if I'm working on a project. I keep note cards, which become part of my inspirational stack where I record quick thoughts. Some of those thoughts later appear in books, blogs, or songs. With fitness, short and consistent is better than long or non-existent!

Fiscal: Your Budget

Some women at halftime are used to keeping good records and know their exact financial status. Others have left that responsibility to a spouse, feeling apprehensive about one day becoming the sole financial administrator of their households. Still others may dabble but are looking at a bleak future with rising health costs and many unknowns. Whatever the situation, most women realize that understanding and managing finances are extremely important skills for their futures. Facing the care of parents is also a growing concern. One stark reality we are facing in our family is the expensive cost of home elder care.

Whatever fiscal system a woman has in place, my encouragement is to at least have a structure and plan, including effective communication with other family members. For those who need help in this area, it is worth pursuing a trusted advisor, which is always my first recommendation.

As a creative soul, I keep my finances balanced and pay for all projects as I run my business, but getting more deeply into financial planning makes my head spin. My husband takes care of the more complicated financial matters, but we communicate often about our family decisions. I know where essential documents are filed and have access to loan details, insurance policies, and online passwords. He has also given me basic information of what to look for in an advisor.

That communication is vital, so we should not put it off but become informed now for decision making later. It's difficult to predict what the financial markets will do for future investments or how technology will bring changes in the job market. However, by defining our expertise and competency with the addition of building skills based upon our competency, we will be better equipped to adapt to life's challenges.

> *A carefully crafted budget should include not only our finances, but also our time.*

Some at halftime have the opportunity to promote a worthy cause without monetary remuneration. Whatever the situation, we must have the mindset that time equals money, whether we get paid in dollars or with the reward of helping others. Thus, a carefully crafted budget should include not only our finances but also our time, which is one of our most valuable resources but often the most wasted.

No one is able to predict how much sand is left in life's hourglass. When budgeting time, it is a good idea to spend moments enjoying our surroundings, appreciating those we love, and acknowledging our own worthiness. Money is not an end but only a means; we also can buy time by appreciating each moment with its inherent blessings. Time is short, so we must spend our moments wisely.

Physical: Your Brain

How can we invest in our brains to keep them sharp? After watching my father-in-law's mind slowly disintegrate, leaving him a shell of his former intellectual self, I have wondered if hope remains for nurturing a memory that won't burn to ashes of dementia. Yet, those thoughts should not keep me from investing intellectually as a lifelong learner. Some experts wonder if stress causes the early onset of dementia. People vary widely in their abilities to cope with stressful events, but we do know that stress affects the body as well as the mind. However, there are relatively few well-controlled studies on the effect of stress relating to Alzheimer's and dementia.[53]

Regardless of our risks of developing dementia with age, it is important to nurture a positive outlook, stimulating our minds by learning, reading, and interaction with others. By doing so, the myelin sheath stays active and continues to fire synapses in our brains. Myelin is a whitish covering that insulates nerve fibers connecting neurons. This nerve network can help us reinforce good habits. It is actually a powerful method to change mindsets and mental code. As impulses, or neurons move faster and faster with repetition, the myelin builds and strengthens. With that strengthening, we are actually producing new neurons to reshape certain areas of the brain. That process is known as neuroplasticity. Further, in neurogenesis, the brain actually creates new neurons.[54]

Strengthening the myelin sheath applies to most any type of habit and routine.

According to a 2018 study from Columbia University, brain cells are continuously added to our brains even when we reach our 70s. This was revealed from investigating the postmortem brains of twenty-eight individuals between age fourteen and seventy-nine. The results showed that for all age groups, the hippocampus, *(area dealing with memory)*, shows new developing neurons. Dr. Laura Boldrini, a research scientist at Columbia, said that new neurons were present in older brains, but they make fewer connections than those in younger brains. This is because of fewer proteins and reduction in blood vessels as people got older.[55]

Relating this to habits, I believe our actual brain signals can change to create desire and craving for a different substance according to our defined lifestyle and outcome. Developing neurons and strengthening the myelin sheath applies to any habit and routine, not limited by age. For a fit lifestyle, focus on the feeling you get after an invigorating walk or use of weights. We can put that routine in our schedule and improve our mental attitude, strengthening our myelin sheath with an *I can* attitude.

> *Our actual brain signals can change to create desire and craving for a different substance according to our defined lifestyle and outcome.*

Relational: Reflection and Contemplation

Eastern religions explore the possibilities of one's personality with self-realization. **Hinduism** looks for the true self, **Buddhism** seeks the separate self, and the **Western World** focuses mostly on humanistic, psychological growth. We live in a society of self; taking selfies, self-image, self-promotion and self-confidence.

As we look inside ourselves, we may find a vacuum. I believe there is a God-shaped vacuum inside every person, so true actualization is only fulfilled when supplied by a supreme being. A truth including a higher power brings several cables of success together. Those cables include our purpose and mission and also our habits. A higher power is necessary to evoke authentic and true change. Our routine should include time to reflect, explore, and contemplate on that truth.

> *A higher power is necessary to evoke authentic and true change.*

The brain is a powerful muscle, and like most muscles, needs exercise. How many books have we read this year? How many hours do we spend watching shows on Netflix or YouTube, compared to the moments we spend keeping our mind sharp learning a new skill? We are worth investing in. As we strengthen our habits cable, we realize that our hardest sell will be to ourselves. It's easier to focus on everything else; work, home, children or spouse. However, feeding and nourishing our goals creates life balance. To pursue an ideal lifestyle is not selfish; it's important. In fact, it's more self-serving to ignore our own routines and behaviors, as negative habits will bring undesirable consequences for our entire family.

At this life stage, my husband and I care for aging parents, so we have faced the stark reality that what we ignore now will be managed later by our children. As a result, I am working toward a less complicated life, by purging household goods more often and attending to financial records on a regular basis. My hope is that in my elderly stages, there will be less for my children to manage. No one can control the future, but we can tend to the details of today.

In summary, good habits don't just include a program but a desire. We can change our lifestyles and mindsets because we are worth it! Our improvement means a better life for our families as well.

*No one can control the future,
but we can tend to the details of today.*

THE RHYTHM OF LIFE

"I Got Rhythm" is a song composed by George and Ira Gershwin, published in 1930, which became a jazz standard. It's chord changes became the foundation for many other jazz tunes, perfect for jazz improvisers.

Many who have grown up trained in classical music are challenged with jazz or pop rhythms and chord changes. Developing an inner clock, or sense of personal rhythm to improvise outside a strict classical form is not easy for an exacting classical player. I have coached many students on developing a feeling of rhythm, requiring them to create a count-off for a song, just as they would bring in a band. This is also similar to a count-off for a dance routine with 5 – 6 – 7 – 8.

In the same way, developing and maintaining good habits takes on a distinct rhythm. Almost subconsciously I create a monthly rhythm, which then breaks down to a weekly rhythm of projects. There is enough flexibility built into the schedule to expand on what is necessary and pull back on what is less urgent.

Just like a steady schedule, a band will keep the beat consistent and even, letting the soloist gain freedom and expand, or slow down a phrase for impact, always coming back to the main established beat. When a soloist extends a phrase, stretching it or speeding it up, we can visualize pulling a piece of taffy or stretching a rubber band. Both materials expand, but then return to a normal state.

Our schedules will do the same. There are times when multiple activities make one feel stretched, taught and frantic. However, a steady schedule, just as a steady beat, maintains an even rhythm. That steady schedule allows one the freedom to improvise more effectively. As we identify, then keep the end goal in mind for projects and deadlines, it is easier to stretch when necessary as we know there will be a time to get back to a calm, regular routine.

The included charts will help to establish a normal monthly and weekly rhythm. First, focus on the main goals and projects for the month. We have not taken a deep dive into long-term or short-term goals in this book, but as we plan our year, months and weeks, our mission and purpose statements provide the direction to establish those goals.

IMPORTANCE OF ROUTINE

In the past few months as my father has been very ill, I have continued learning from him about the importance of routine. Watching him go through his daily personal tasks has brought back memories of him completing a detailed checklist before flying his low-winged Piper airplane. When constructing a building, he created detailed lists and gathered his tools the night before, preparing for workers that would need them first thing in the morning.

His life has been one of routine, yet flexibility. Watching him go through the motions of brushing his teeth, then wetting the comb to go through his hair, *(at least on the sides and back)* and even put on deodorant before going to bed kept him moving forward even while very ill. His routine truly was his management tool. It not only helped him manage business, but a robust life.

When looking ahead, creating a schedule that fits our lifestyle, we may block out days or parts of days for specific projects or travel. However, our schedule should still contain the main projects to be completed. With a steady rhythm and routine, along with a bit of improvisation and flexibility, what feels insurmountable can be accomplished.

1. MONTHLY RHYTHM

What is not completed in week 1 is carried over to week 2 and so on.

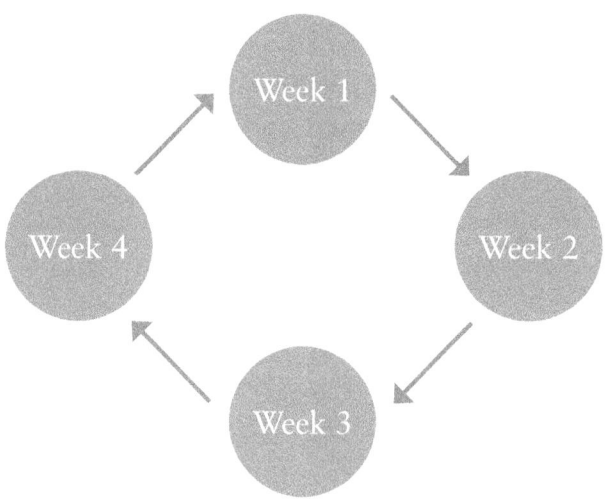

Month

Week 1 main project: _____

Week 2 main project: _____

Week 3 main project: _____

Week 4 main project: _____

2. WEEKLY RHYTHM

What is not completed in day 1 is carried over to day 2 and so on. Decide what you want your schedule to look like and how many days to schedule your work. Block out days or weekends if desired.

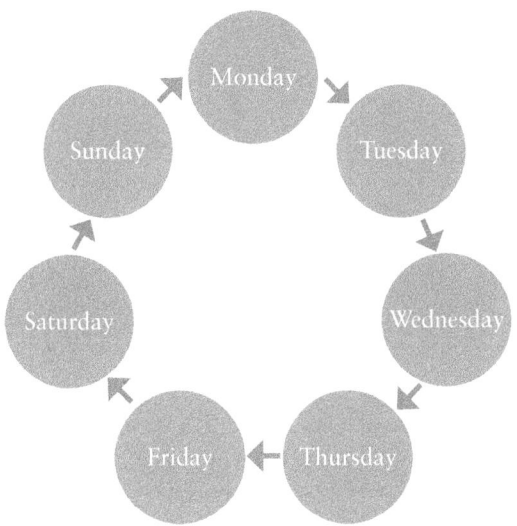

Day

Week 1 main project: _____

Week 2 main project: _____

To do: _____

To do: _____

To do: _____

To do: _____

3. HABITS

This chart can be filled out monthly or even weekly if desired. It is meant to help you set achievable short-term goals for physical, fiscal and spiritual areas of your life.

Sleep
Diet
Exercise
Debt
Finances
Higher Power

APPLICATION

Do you have some powerhouse habits you have created? Name those here, or brainstorm at least one you can start right away.

_____

_____

How have you encountered cheap ambition in your life and what was the result?

_____

_____

What steps are you taking to create authentic ambition, focusing on a true expert status?

_____

_____

Differentiate technical versus adaptive approaches and how they both apply in your life.

- Technical approach

    _____

    _____

- Adaptive approach

    _____

    _____

Name some healthy physical habits you plan to put in place or improve:

- Sleep

  _____

  _____

- Diet

  _____

  _____

- Exercise

  _____

  _____

What fiscal habit will you implement or improve?

- Debt

  _____

  _____

- Financial Advisor

  _____

  _____

What, if any, higher power decision do you need to make?

_____

_____

SEVEN

Relationships Cable

When climbing, to mitigate the risk of falling on steep, hard snow or slipping into a crevasse, it is essential for climbers to join a rope team. These teams usually consist of two to four people. The guiding principle for the rope teams is to keep the rope taught throughout the climb. Too much slack poses a risk for the team.[56] If the ropes are not tight enough, a climber can fall and may even pull others down with him. Each member must be aware of and value the principles of rope climbing.

Good climbing partners are important for safety and confidence by pushing fellow climbers to do and be their best. The same principle is true in life, with coworkers, clients, and especially with marriage partnerships.

Marriages and the families they produce form the backbone of our society. We treasure them and understand their significance as seen in the public interest of the recent royal wedding of Prince Harry and Meghan Markle on May 19, 2018. The ratings company said twenty-nine million people tuned in to view the ceremony along with the couple's carriage procession through Windsor. In fact, fifteen different broadcast and cable networks covered the event.[57] The world was fascinated not only with royalty, but the dresses, the hats, the guests and the flowers. The fairy-tale couple seemed fortunate enough to live happily ever after.

These ceremonies often include common features: wedding songs, vows, trumpet fanfares, expensive buffets, horse-drawn carriages, and ice sculptures. I have attended, or participated as a professional musician, in hundreds of weddings with those elements. A marriage ceremony is an important rite of passage. When the bride and groom say, " I do," a profound change occurs. A woman joins her life with another human being, different from her in more ways than she can imagine. In this respect, I think God has a sense of humor!

After that ceremony, whether simple or extravagant, change happens—it will transpire whether or not we're prepared. During halftime, a surprising transformation also may arise in relationships when a spouse's "I do" becomes, "I don't." Marriage counselors say most problems couples face start with an inability to grow and change, at least with one of the partners. These alterations often occur during halftime.

This circumstance is understandable. When a couple is raising children together, much of their focus and purpose is centered on growing those children into responsible adults. It's a bucket-load of work with alternating night duty, diaper changes, then school projects and missed curfews. As the children grow to adulthood, the object of a couple's attention changes as their focus and energy are then redefined. A single parent also faces similar adjustments, with or without the involvement of an ex-spouse.

> *During halftime, a surprising transformation may arise in relationships when a person's "I do" becomes, "I don't."*

Contending with relationships is a lot like riding a roller coaster. There are twists, turns, and surprising jolts. Some embrace those sudden spirals with ebullience. Others just brace themselves with eyes closed, knuckles white as they hang on, waiting for the air brakes to end their peril. Even though there are twists and turns in relationships at halftime, there's no need to panic. Such alterations are normal and can be met with confidence and expectancy, especially when we establish a few ground rules and employ astute discernment. We have to embrace the "morph."

MORPHING

In computer animation, the term *morphing* describes an image that is changed from one shape to another in gradual steps. Life has its morphing stages too. Whether married or single, an entrepreneur, office worker, or a non-profit leader, morphing relationships occur often at halftime. With changing priorities that redefine purpose, certain friendships, relationships and business contacts will also shift. Some will become less important while others become more so.

> *With changing priorities that redefine purpose, certain friendships, relationships and business contacts will also shift.*

Defining how those relationships will look and how they can morph with small gradual steps is a thought-provoking prospect. The transformation of a caterpillar to a butterfly is a process described by the Greek word *metamorphosis*. The modification from caterpillar to butterfly materializes more quickly than in humans, but the principle is the same; it is good to take gradual steps during metamorphosis. However, even those incremental revisions will push many out of their comfort zones.

When I was entering my halftime years, I did not recognize some of the natural changes occurring in my body. Compared to others, who were experiencing hot flashes and mood fluctuations, I felt fine, so I didn't realize I was also changing. Both my sisters, who were undergoing their share of adjustments, were jealous of my so-called normalcy. Looking back, I realize that I dismissed some of the signs because I didn't equate them with a new life stage. Was I in denial?

After waking up soaking wet from night sweats, I thought I was hot from too many blankets on my bed. At the change in my monthly cycle, I didn't recognize that my husband and I didn't have as much to talk about. For me, the changes were subtle, which can actually be dangerous. Ignoring my feelings rather than evaluating them could have led to my feeling alienation, bitterness, and anger. Such held-in feelings have the power to drive wedges between people, complicating their ability to communicate.

DEFINE RELATIONSHIPS

Thus, life changes can bring changes in relationships. So one of the first steps is to define relationships. As life stages evolve, we may face the following relationship dilemmas:

- You're not the same person I married.
- I don't love you anymore.
- We have nothing in common any more.
- We never have time to get together!
- I'm not sure I can work with you anymore.

Those statements reveal common dilemmas that one may encounter when relating to a spouse, friend, or coworker. Maybe it's we and not the other people who have become different. Priorities change; jobs change; even our spiritual lives change. Possibly our extroverted "life of the party" personality has transformed into a more subdued introverted one, who craves alone time.

Understanding our basic personalities helps us ride waves of change. We can get as detailed as we wish, but even perceiving the basics can be freeing. As we seek to understand ourselves, it's worth deciding and defining who we would like to have or keep in our close circle of contacts. If we were fleeing a sinking ship, who would be in our life rafts? Those people are our closest connections.

> *If we were on a sinking ship, who would*
> *be in our life raft? Those people are*
> *our closest circle of connections.*

However, we can't forget the many others, still on that ship, who are valuable to us in different ways. Many are tempted to retreat in isolation when change, adjustments and revisions occur. This is not only dangerous socially but physically. We need each other, and the value of healthy relationships increases with the lengthening shadows of time. So it is important to take time to define our closest relationships, then nurture them.

> *We need each other, and the value of healthy relationships*
> *increases with the lengthening shadows of time.*

RELATIONSHIP CIRCLES

Who is in our life-raft? How we define the connections in that inner circle depends on us. We will naturally have people closest to us, like family members, a spouse or lifelong friends. But as our work, life, and purpose change, even those relationships alter. Some will remain in our inner circles while others will move to the expanded circles of our lives.

Casual friendships and social interactions play an important part in networking and building businesses. They are also good for mastermind groups to help brainstorm current and future goals. Even though every friend will not be a close associate or colleague, the interaction with others is important. In a study of 2,300 men surviving a heart attack, those who were socially isolated with high stress experienced four to six times the risk of death than those with social interaction and a lower stress level.[58] Everyone needs connections of some sort.

That statistic is also relevant for woman since heart disease is currently the number one killer of females, followed by cancer. Further, connection with others must be face-to-face and person-to-person rather than a "Facebook friend." Relationships that are as fake as a movie set have increased with the rise of social media. Individuals may "feel" connected to their social media cohorts, but such relationships rely merely on a paper-thin base that crumbles easily in *Twitterland* and *Instagramality*. Isolation increases as face-to-face contact is replaced by technological communication. Simply answering texts and connecting virtually shortchanges the value a human touch and interaction.

> *Individuals may "feel" connected to their social media cohorts, but such relationships rely merely on a paper-thin base that crumbles easily in Twitterland and Instagramality.*

Substantial studies reveal that connection with friends or relatives is one of the best activities for staving off dementia. It will at least reduce the onset and that should be enough for most to heed the warning![59] Involvement in situations and events where people can interact and be inspired is not easy for many. In fact, for some creative souls, hibernating at home in a comfortable cave becomes the easier choice.

At mid-life, it is important to take stock of our relationships to see how they can be improved. We can start by creating a list, defining those in our various relationship circles, including our inner circle, then those who are not in our life rafts, but still important; and last, our outer circle of contacts, including professional colleagues. Establishing this list will take time but will also reveal ways we can expand our circle of influence, friendships, and business opportunities. Further, we may decide we need to expand our circles. If we need to meet more people, various multi-generational groups can provide an additional pool of resources for our community circles.

> *Establishing our list of contacts will reveal ways we can expand our circle of influence, friendships and even business opportunities.*

CONNECTIONS AND GROUPS

Most understand that dividends play an important part in one's finances by adding value to an investor's portfolio. Similarly, activities that make us laugh, think, or listen add health benefits. So it follows that stretching beyond our comfort zones or sameness provides an even healthier dividend.

Sometimes, change requires our imaginations, as we observe when children play. Those of us with grandchildren often see firsthand how children use their imaginations, transforming a simple object into the theme for a complete story. I've watched children make cars out of ordinary Lincoln Logs. It looked nothing like a car to me, but after they described it in detail, I understood their visionary creation.

Often in adulthood, many jobs or minor tasks require us to close off imagination and experimentation because we face deadlines and project restrictions. Taking time out to play and to create may feel strange if we do not exercise those powers from time to time. There will always be more projects, more emergencies, more work, and more books to read. All are good, but not to the exclusion of healthy social interaction and relaxation. Taking time for this creativity and connection can be a challenge in my life as I'm quite project-driven.

> *Taking time out to play and create will feel strange if we do not exercise those powers from time to time.*

However, I have found that taking a break for creative inspiration is worth the risk. For example, I have actually enrolled in classes in Comedy Improvisation. Admittedly, before each session, I often questioned myself:

- You are not getting any better. Why keep trying?
- Do you really have time for this? You're writing a new book!
- Comedy? What are you thinking? You'll never use this!

Yet those classes allowed me to laugh at myself. I left happier by recalling how the whole group worked together in various scenes. So I not only made new friends with those whose lives are different from mine, but also, I felt encouraged to have fun and engage in imaginary comic scenes.

It is dangerous to live a scripted, habitual life. Deeply engrained routines in activities and even in meal choices can lead to monotonous ruts. I took improv classes to develop greater freedom in relating to my audiences, allowing me to move away from a standard script, whether in music or speaking. However, it's not always easy to take a breath and do an impromptu scene, whether in class or in my business. But for all of us, it is important to try. So we must ask ourselves, is there a class or group I can take to expand my thinking? Most communities have organizations that will gladly welcome new attendees. We should challenge ourselves to try something new.

It is dangerous to live a scripted, habitual life.

THE IMPROMPTU LIFE

We may need some improvisational skills since life brings impromptu moments. No one can plan exactly how life's next scene will unfold. In the same way, nor do any of us have expiration dates stamped our foreheads. When the time comes to care for aging parents or engage with boomeranging children, our lives become more complicated. To cope with these changes, we need resources. Tremendous support can be found in church groups, networking groups, even non-profit boards or volunteer organizations. Further, we can find an activity or focus outside our normal scope of work that will interest us.

*No one can plan exactly how life's next scene will unfold.
Nor do any of us have expiration dates
stamped on our foreheads.*

Groups help their members pull together toward a common goal, providing common relationship threads. Even though those group members may not be in our closest circle of friends, they provide necessary connections that benefit our souls, our health and even our businesses. Most know that one of the quickest ways to grow a business is through relationships and referrals. If the faucet of referrals runs dry, we can focus on building new relationships. We can venture outside our current contact network by attending additional events and meetings.

The reality is, as we grow older, our world gets smaller. I learned this first hand while helping my aged mother-in-law. When she moved from her large home to a one-room unit in a care facility, it meant she could only take a few clothes and possessions. All the material goods she accumulated and treasured over decades became irrelevant. More importantly, though, she kept friends, family and valued caregivers. In that respect, she remained rich. It is not too late to build that treasure chest of true friends by expanding our relationships.

To *have* a friend is to *be* a friend, so part of relationship development is to understand and truly care for others, both personally and professionally. After defining our circles of influence, we can show appreciation to those who are closest to us in genuine ways they will understand. We can discern the way they feel valued and acknowledged by defining their love languages.

*It is not too late to build that treasure chest of
true friends by expanding our relationships.*

UNDERSTANDING LOVE LANGUAGES

Even though most people fit in several categories, it has been helpful for me to define the love language of those I care about. In this way,

I can communicate in ways that make others feel understood. This is extremely helpful in business relationships, especially with a worker or colleague who feels unappreciated.

> *Discovering what makes another person feel appreciated or heard eliminates or at least discounts their sense of being misunderstood, ignored, or irrelevant.*

Gary Chapman's book The Five Love Languages,[60] which sold over eleven million copies, contains simple ideas that are both timeless and priceless in application. With those relationships that morph during halftime, discovering what makes another person feel appreciated or heard eliminate or at least discounts their sense of being misunderstood, ignored, or irrelevant. If we are the ones feeling unloved or misunderstood, then defining our own languages is a good starting place. The five languages defined by Chapman are as follows:

Words of Affirmation

We can get beyond ourselves to think about others with a kind word, to creatively express our appreciation. Emails, notecards, phone messages are means to send short, thoughtful messages. To affirm someone is to build them up. So our messages must do that in an honest, succinct way.

Quality time

We shouldn't be in such a rush! My husband likes quality time. Our morning conversations over coffee while practicing the Italian phrases we are learning provide together time. I rush through communication, with short sentences and brief topics, but he likes contemplative pondering. I have learned to appreciate his astuteness, especially as I ramble through issues that I write and blog about.

Receiving Gifts

Our gifts don't need to be large or expensive as a piece of Tiffany jewelry. Even small tokens communicate appreciation to those who love gifts. Additionally, presentation of the gift is also important. One of my sisters always wraps presents with beautiful bows and paper, but she also likes to receive gifts, large or small.

Acts of Service

We can offer our time and effort as an act of service to a family member, friend, or coworker. This is my main love language. So when someone does something for me without being asked, it communicates care, devotion, and consideration for my time. Even a small act signals respect from the giver. Recently, when a member of an organization I lead followed through on responsibilities without a phone call reminder, the message I received was that the person valued my time enough to complete a task without a prompt.

Physical Touch

This love language is transmitted differently between men and women but is important for both. Physical touch goes beyond sexual connotations, especially as it relates to a love language. A pat on the shoulder, fist bump, or even side hug are accepted forms of physical touch for most in our society. However, many individuals in our society are from differing cultures. So it is important to understand those from contrasting traditions, where physical touch may be offensive.

THE KEY CONNECTION: COMMUNICATION

Communication is the key connection in all the love languages. Constructive communication builds relationships. Negative and critical communication alienates and tears down relationships. Halftime is an opportune place to expand and build on current and new contacts by using love languages to heighten conversations and involvement. It's easy to let our worlds grow smaller. However, fewer conversations and mental stimulation can bring loneliness and isolation.

What do we do if our worlds have already shrunk? First, we stop waiting for others to contact us. We should reconnect with friends and colleagues, then expand to other groups and organizations. If it is difficult to enter new spheres, we can find a friend to go with us. If conversation topics are a concern, we can keep up with new trends and ideas beyond politics so we will always have topics of interest.

> *We should reconnect with familiar contacts and then expand to other groups and organizations.*

I admire those of my father's generation who learned to navigate social media and willingly use computers. In fact, my own father's interest and adoption of new technologies has provided us with deeper topics of conversation than merely medical bills and doctor appointments. It also provides laughter as I decipher some of his text messages, sent without proof-reading!

LIFETIME GROUP

Thus, the five languages of love apply to loved ones and acquaintances, both public and personal. These approaches help us to understand others as well as ourselves. This way of communication especially applies to our close circles who are extremely important, as they act as anchors when we hit life's disruptive storms. When I realized a little over ten years ago that I was facing major life changes, I assembled a group of women whom I absolutely trust. I asked four specific friends to join me in my journey, and they have become a part of my lifetime group. Each has been part of my life in different ways, whether from a previous job, a small group I led, or a professional colleague.

Since we share much more than just business when meeting, it's helpful that we all possess similar spiritual beliefs, values, and commitment to our families. We don't meet often. In fact, we're happy if we can meet every three months. But the most important element is that we meet personally. This is not an online group. We hug; we cry, and we pray together. It's not only a lifetime group but a lifeline group.

Women need each other. We can burrow into our cubicles churning out projects harder and faster. We can also busy ourselves with children and grandchildren, making their lives ours. We can make our computers our sole focus. But to share and interact with others, including our peers and acquaintances, is vital to good health, lower stress levels, and even staving off or slowing the onset of dementia.

> *To share and interact with one another is vital to good health, lower stress and even staving off or slowing the onset of dementia.*

If we pursue a lifetime group *(I hope everyone will)*, it is important to choose members carefully. We don't need to be everyone's best friend. Different acquaintances and relationships play various roles in our lives. We may have several groups, including a business mastermind group. This is a valuable resource, once assembled with wisdom and caution, that provides benefits to entrepreneurs or small business owners. Finding the right people can take time, maybe a year or two. Many masterminds meet online, as location is not critical.

> *We don't need to be everyone's best friend.*

Time is one of our most valuable assets. The time we spend with those who are in our closest circles will influence many other parts of our life. Hours spent expanding our relationships will serve as a referral base and common connection to give access to others once inaccessible. Overall, relationships benefit our mental, emotional, and physical health. They are well-worth the effort to maintain in our halftime years and beyond.

*Relationships benefit our mental, emotional,
and physical health.*

RELATIONSHIP CIRCLES

Casual Circle: Friendships
Networking groups, outside work contacts, people in face-to-face meetings.

**Comfort Circle:
Friends, Colleagues, Associates**
Larger group of trusted friends but not in inner circle or on life raft. Mastermind groups, work associates, extended family.

Close Circle
Lifetime group, close family, few trusted colleagues.

Outer Circle: Social Media Groups
Facebook friends, Instagram, Twitter and newsletter contacts.

APPLICATION

Define an important relationship in your life. *(spouse, special friend, colleague, or child)*
_____
_____

Do you consider yourself an introvert or extravert and why? *(Has this changed during halftime?)*
_____
_____

Who are the people you would include in your life raft?
_____
_____

Define your personal love language(s).
_____
_____

In what ways can you encourage at least one of your important relationships by using a love language?
_____
_____

Take some time to define some of the people in your relationship circles on the previous page.
_____
_____

RELATIONSHIPS CABLE

Close Circle:	1. Language
1.	
2.	2. Language
3.	3. Language

Comfort Circle:	1. Language
1.	
2.	2. Language
3.	3. Language

Casual Circle	Outer Circle
1.	1.
2.	2.
3.	3.

EIGHT

Reaching Your Summit

Congratulations! We have now gone through all the cables of success and are standing at the top of our individual Hero Mountains™. We're a little breathless as we look at the prospects before us. The view is amazing as we deeply gulp the mountain air. We feel satisfaction and contentment as we stand at the summit with a renewed perspective, but we realize there must be more to come.

In 1969, the song, **"Is That All There Is?"** became Peggy Lee's[61] first top 40 pop hit. The lyrics reflect a person who is disillusioned with life events, ones that should have provided mountaintop experiences. Even death would be a disappointment to this individual. Where do we go from the highest mountain peak? The song suggests disillusionment and disenchantment derive from the journey. It seems the only path left is downhill. Likewise, we may also sense loss or disappointment as we reach our personal summits.

What about a misstep? We may develop a fear of falling hard and fast in life's second half. However, if the climbing cables of success are strong, fortified with healthy habits and purpose statements, we can have hope and positive momentum for our future strides. Our journeys do not end by merely reaching the top.

> *If the climbing cables of success are strong, fortified with healthy habits and purpose statements, there is hope and positive momentum for our future strides.*

Others may relay mixed messages of both congratulations and warnings once we complete our journeys. For example, I remember that after completing my graduate recital and thesis, a colleague warned that I would probably face depression and feel letdown after earning my degree. It was as if he expected me to tumble off my mountaintop experience.

His warning confused me since I came from a performance and competition background. I did not approach every opportunity, whether a concert date or completion of a new composition, as an anticlimax. Instead, I carried the mindset that each completion was an opportunity to grow and move forward. Every competition and performance provided chances to take my skills to new levels. That view propelled me forward, so that I welcomed new challenges rather than merely basking in the achievement of completed ones.

IS THAT ALL THERE IS?

As we reach summits of reevaluation and recharging, we can apply a similar principle and awareness. While we have taken a giant step in reaching one summit, there are more hills to climb. Therefore, with our cables of success solidly in place, these new challenges will not be as difficult or rocky. Just as the earth rotates on its axis, bringing new sunrises and sunsets, our lives also pivot, revolve, and adjust. Change comes with the close of each day or chapter of our lives, so there is fresh opportunity beginning with every breaking dawn.

*Just as the earth rotates on its axis, bringing new
sunrises and sunsets, our lives also
pivot, revolve, and adjust.*

In her 2017 TEDWomen talk, psychologist Susan David, surveyed over 70,000 people regarding courage. She found in a third of the responses people either judge themselves for having negative emotions or actively try to push aside those adverse feelings. Many responders did not want to try because they feared that disappointment or disenchantment would haunt them. Such disillusionment leads individuals to live out the message of **"Is That all There Is?"**

What was Susan's David's answer? She explained that such respondents have dead people's goals! For only dead people are free of unwanted or inconvenient feelings. They never endure the stress or broken heartedness or disappointment that comes with failure. David says, "Discomfort is the price of admission to a meaningful life."[62]

*Change comes with the close of each day or
chapter of our lives, and there is fresh opportunity
beginning with every breaking dawn.*

Susan's main point is that life naturally brings disappointment. In my grad school situation, I knew discouragement was possible after achieving the high of completing my thesis and recital to earn the graduate degree that followed. I understood the euphoria, then letdown, having faced those feelings many times throughout my performance career. Yet I did not let those feelings steal my joy in finishing an admirable task. That exercise became an attitude I repeatedly practiced. I understood that the recital and thesis did not represent the end of my academic or professional journey. Indeed, they were just a beginning.

Much in my life has changed since that early achievement. Soon afterward, I became pregnant with our first son. My new norm became a fast-paced life where I balanced a career while caring for my husband and three sons. Those challenges became my new norm. In speaking of change, John F. Kennedy, the thirty-fifth U.S. President, once said, "Change is the law of life. And those who look only to the past or present are certain to miss the future."[63]

LOOKING TO THE FUTURE

One thing is sure: the world is changing at an increasing pace. In an average minute, Facebook receives 900,000 logins; more than 450,000 Tweets are posted; 156 million emails are read, and 15 million texts are sent. We are essentially doubling the amount of data created in the world every two years.[64]

Amongst the advent of self-driving smart cars with programmed destinations, computers that process faster than the human mind can comprehend, and a wide range of industries impacted by automation, the mindset of enjoying the present, yet focusing on the future is fundamental to a healthy mental code.

Remember Disney's **Carousel of Progress**? What used to be a main attraction at Disneyland Resorts is now a faint memory. The **Carousel** was created by Walt Disney for the 1964-65 New York World's Fair with the classic song, **"There's a Great Big Beautiful Tomorrow."** It was a must-see attraction every time I visited Disneyland while growing up. The Carousel actually underwent many revisions in Disneyland Park until it closed for good in 2001.

Yet that closed door opened more opportunity for new attractions relevant for a new age. Similarly, just because some gateways of our pasts are now closed or closing, it's no time to panic. It is actually a time to embrace change since advances in automation, robotics, and technology are moving at light speed.

> *Just because some gateways of our pasts are now closed or closing, it's no time to panic.*

AUTOMATION

Robots will not take over the world. They only try to do that in the movies. In fact, robots create additional need for human interaction. Automation is best used to take over rote jobs, freeing up the time and creative energy for us to use other skills. Take calculators, for example. I rarely use mental math to add or multiply large numbers anymore because a small device will do the computations for me.

Every time the sprinklers go on around our home, I think *automation!* Those system timers free us to work in other areas of our yard and garden while saving water. However, those timers do need programing, or they will not work. In the same way, learning how to best use additional automation will open new doors of opportunity, especially for women.

Our developed skills, career experience, and freedom at halftime will generate additional opportunity in select areas. We cannot let anyone convince us otherwise. To maximize our opportunities, we can't back away from technology. We don't have to learn how to code or grasp engineering skills. Online programs abound with a growing number of areas in technology for the development of skills in our time and space.

> *Our developed skills, life and career experience, and freedom at halftime will generate additional opportunity in select areas.*

To keep up with technologies that I can use, my practice is to read one tech blog a week as well as listen to a podcast focusing on tech. Recently, I pay more attention to current posts and events as I guide others. If I find even one small nugget of helpful information, it is worth the time for me to read or listen.

Focusing on our internal strengths, mindsets, relationships and purpose will help us develop our external skills. Working from the inside out will help us adjust with a calm reassurance and determined mindset. Even when plodding stubbornly through necessary changes, we can face the eye of the storm, secure and calm in knowing who we are and where we are going. Our ship won't capsize!

Focusing on our internal strengths, mindsets, relationships and purpose will help us develop our external skills.

OUR INNER RUDDER

In the same way that a rudder steers a ship, our inner rudder controls our life's direction and guides our courses. It's an inner counselor—our soul, spirit, and awareness—that guides our actions and feelings. That internal awareness is linked to a woman's intuition, a deep-seated insight that feeds on knowledge, experience, and instinct. Yet intuition is not based on these aspects alone.

Intuition and guidance are also derived from beliefs. I have a strong belief in the higher power of a personal God. I also believe prayer and reflection are important parts of every person's journey. True peace doesn't come from some regulatory program or sanction, but from an inner decision and guidance. There are many who reject any sense of spirituality, but when faced with a major crisis, they realize there is more to life than what is only visible or tangible.

True peace doesn't come from some sort of regulatory program or sanction but from an inner decision and guidance.

We all understand uncontrolled panic. It happens in those times where we find ourselves in the middle of a confusing and threatening dream. We are silenced by the unvoiced scream where our cries expel in slow motion, as though screaming in quicksand. That same feeling arises amidst crisis and change. Our emotional waters become muddy, sludgy, and swampy. Panic and fear bring thoughts of flight. Yet we are unable to move forward. When faced with feelings of impending disaster, we need help.

POWER GREATER THAN OURSELVES

During such desperate times, it is crucial to seek a power greater than ourselves. When I marvel at the formation of the mountains, am inspired by the pounding of the waves on a seashore, or sit mesmerized at the expansive, infinite star-filled sky, I am awed. The intricacies of nature could not have appeared with a large explosion or big bang.

Likewise, the human body is equally awe-inspiring. Our hands alone contain twenty-seven bones. When I move my fingers across piano keys, I take it for granted that they will all move in sync. For most, hands and feet move in a rhythm that allows us to walk and hold objects. The intricate signals, connections, and triggers for movement do not just happen randomly. They presuppose a designer. In the same way, we could not say all the pieces of a watch or timepiece *(remember those?)* just gathered together to work perfectly in sync on their own power. There must be a designer if a design exists.

For a simpler explanation, Michael Behe in his book *Darwin's Black Box,* writes of the function of the mousetrap. It is to immobilize a mouse, so it can't chew through sacks of flour or electrical cords. [65] I have direct experience with mousetraps since I live close to the mountains where I contend with rodents. A basic wooden trap consists of the following parts: a platform, holding bar, catch, spring and hammer. If one part is missing, the trap will not work. In fact, if one part is immobilized the trap will fail. Even though there are many other examples of traps, the simplicity of the mousetrap design illustrates the importance of fabrication and function. It is simple but effective.

IMPORTANCE OF DESIGN

The design of a trap pales in comparison with the universe, the body, and even a timepiece, yet the principle holds true. In his book, Behe was writing on the implications of biochemistry's discoveries since

Darwin's research in 1859. Understandably, since 1859, there have been tremendous advances in molecular biology, biochemistry, and genetics. With those advances, the complexity of the design grows in magnitude and significance. Those intricacies are difficult to explain from a mere evolutionary process. There had to be a designer.

When I think of the significance and magnitude of that designer, my thoughts turn to a God who is more creative and powerful than I can imagine. Thus, those thoughts aren't based on some blind faith. The ultimate reality of God puts life in perspective. There is no way we can comprehend all that happens in a lifetime. But as the late Billy Graham said, "When you're prepared to die, you're prepared to live."[66]

When the waters are muddy, and we're standing at the foot of Hero Mountain, we can take heart. There is power and help for the climb both physically and spiritually. We can prepare for the ascent with the proper tools and take one step at a time. All the while, we reflect on the significance of our uniqueness and surround ourselves with those who will help and encourage us on the journey. Then, we begin. Remember, if we never start, we'll definitely never finish!

This book materialized from my experience at my own life's halftime. In the past few years, I have climbed my own Hero Mountain™, and I keep climbing new hills with my various cables and tools firmly in place. Women all over the world will experience their own life's halftime period in unique ways. My hope is that this book will give many women a strong start in scaling their own Hero Mountain successfully. With that objective, I will have fulfilled part of my purpose. Let's climb on!

LET'S APPLY ALL THIS

To summarize, take time to write a few sentences or application action points for each area of Hero Mountain®:

Define Your Base	Where you are right now: *(Stuck, lost, incompetent, fearful?)*	Action needed to move forward:
Mindset Cable	What Head Trash are you facing? *(incompetent, can't learn tech, failure?)*	Action needed to move forward:
Purpose/Passion Cable	Your Mission Statement:	What will it help you do?
Competency Cable	One of Your Core Strengths:	How will you apply this to the future?

Skills Cable	What are two skills you will develop?	Action needed to move forward:
Habits Cable	What area do you desire to build expert status?	Action needed to move forward:
Relationships Cable	Define your Close Circle:	What changes do you need to make?
Your Summit	Your response to, "Is that all there is?"	How will your future change?

Revisit this chart from time to time to re-evaluate and update. As the seasons of your life bring change, your responses and actions will also change slightly.

INDEX

A
adaptive, 100-106, 119
adjustment, xi, 5, 101, 122-3, 125
Alzheimer's, 19, 111, 158-9
amygdala, 20
anchor, 11, 71, 84-5, 95, 132
assessment, xii, 4-5, 12, 15, 20, 42, 47, 52, 100
authenticity, 39

B
baby boomer, 45, 96, 156
baggage, 8
Billy Graham, 146, 159
blood sugar, 105-6
Buddhism, 112

C
carabiner, 39, 43-5
Charles Duhigg, 34, 101, 156, 158
cheap ambition, 97-100, 119
close circle, 125, 127, 129, 132-3, 135, 137, 148
comfort zone, 33-4, 123, 127
comparison, 12, 87, 145
compass, x, 29, 34-5, 46
competency bank, 73-5, 77, 85, 87, 90

core competency, xiv, 40-1, 43-7, 55-6, 59, 61, 63, 65, 73-4, 147
crystallized intelligence, 75

D
Darwin, 145-6, 159
defeatist, 12, 94
Dementia, 19, 110-11, 126, 133, 158
diplomat, 71-3, 78
disruptive, xii, 132
distinctiveness, 82-3
dividend, 127
dopamine, 105
doubt, 43-4, 51-2
dynamic, iv, 15-6, 25-6, 94

E
emotional response, 102
extravert, 42-3, 136

F
Facebook, 12, 126, 135, 142
fear, xiii, 8-11, 33-4, 37, 40, 44, 52, 57, 78, 80, 85, 108, 139, 141, 144, 147
flexibility, 27, 83, 114,5
foundation, 40, 74-5, 97, 100, 113, 158
franchise, 74-6, 157

G

Gary Chapman, 130, 159
goal, iv, 6-7, 11, 15, 25, 27, 29-30, 35, 46, 71, 77-8, 80, 82-3, 85, 89-90, 93-5, 98-100, 102-3, 113-4, 118, 125, 129, 141, 151
God-shaped vacuum, 112

H

habits, vii, xiv, 16, 27, 44, 84, 87, 93-101, 103-5, 107, 109, 111-3, 115, 117-20, 139-40, 148, 157
halftime brain, 19-21, 31, 33, 35, 54, 58, 66, 70, 85, 94, 104-5, 110, 112
higher power, xiv, 112, 118, 120, 144
Hinduism, 112
hippocampus, 111
hormones, 18-9
humor, x, 16, 18, 29, 73, 96, 122, 157

I

ideal lifestyle, 113
immune system, 18
Instagram, 12, 126, 135
introvert, 42-3, 124, 136, 156
irrelevant, xii, 2, 31, 74, 85, 130
isolation, 125-6, 132

J

Josh Groban, 43, 156
journal, 13, 16, 157

L

legacy, 28
life raft, 125-6, 135-6
lifelong learning, 19, 21-2, 27, 82
lifestyle, 19, 45, 51, 53, 62, 69, 95, 99, 101-3, 106-7, 111-3, 115
lifetime group, ix, 132-3, 135
longevity, 18
love language, 129-132, 136, 159

M

martyrdom, 14, 18
Michael Behe, 145, 159
Michael Phelps, 93-4, 157
mid-life, 2-4, 10, 20, 31, 36, 73, 86, 93, 97, 126
mission statement, 25, 27, 29-30, 33-6, 38, 40, 53-4, 63, 114, 147
mommy-brain, 19-20
Mont Blanc, 8, 155
morph, 123, 130
Multiple Sclerosis, 72
myelin sheath, 111-2

N

necessary ambition, 99-100
negative self-talk, xii, xiii, 10, 12, 15-6, 51
negativity, 8, 11, 44
neuron, 111
neurotransmitter, 105
nutrition, 99

O

optimized mentality, 15

P

panic, 10, 16, 33, 78, 81, 123, 142, 144
paralyzed, 44
personality, 26, 39, 40-2, 112, 124
Philip Simmons, 17, 155
positive thinking, 21, 98, 100
possibilities, 41, 43, 48, 51-3, 55,-6, 66, 70, 77, 80, 112
proficiency, 82, 98

R

re-strategize, 6, 9
referrals, 36, 129
reflection, 77-8, 103, 112, 144
reinvent, xii, 56, 71, 78, 84, 98, 151
rhythm, 113-7, 145
Roger Williams, 84
routine, xiv, 14, 17, 19, 57, 84, 99-101, 103-5, 107-9, 111-5, 128

S

scene, 4, 8, 10, 29, 39, 52, 128-9
schedule, 27, 57, 67, 70, 77, 95, 99, 104, 112, 114-5, 117
Scott Hamilton, 96-7
Shaun White, 15, 155
shifting gears, 9
Shirley Temple, 71-3, 78, 83, 157
sleep, 83, 94, 99, 103-4, 118, 120, 158

social media, 12, 14, 126, 132, 135
soft skills, 33, 47, 51, 55, 58, 60, 62, 85, 88, 90, 156
Spangler Effect, 96
spiritual life, 99, 118, 124
static, 25-6, 30, 86
stress, 10, 16, 18, 22, 26, 36, 40, 44, 77, 82, 110-22, 125, 133, 141, 158
stuck, xi, xiii, 11, 15, 31, 56, 84, 99, 147, 151, 153
superman, 7-8, 155
Supreme being, 112

T

technical, 31-4, 38, 53, 62, 74-5, 79, 85, 100-3, 106, 119
technology, 85, 90-1, 110, 142-3, 159
thankfulness, 16, 19, 21-2
Tony Bennett, 84
transform(ation), 20, 52, 99, 101, 122-4, 127
trigger, 20, 33-4, 101, 105, 145

V

victim mentality, 12, 15, 22

W

Warren Buffet, 77, 87
Western World, 112

ABOUT DEBORAH

Deborah Johnson, M.A., is an international award-winning music artist, author, speaker and national media commentator. She helps others get unstuck with mindsets to reinvent their life and reach expansive goals. Up for multiple GRAMMY Awards and spending over 20 years in the entertainment industry, she's an expert on how to constantly reinvent yourself in a gig-economy. She is also the 2018-2019 President of the National Speakers Association, Los Angeles Chapter.

Her ability to relate to a multi-generational audience doesn't merely come from her educational degrees, but also from her natural abilities and varied experience. Deborah has written three full-length staged musicals and successfully produced two of them as World-Premieres, working with a varied cast of characters and temperaments. She has also successfully hosted and curated artist showcase rooms across the U.S., working on both sides of the fence, with agents and artist teams.

With over two dozen albums, books and hundreds of songs, Deborah understands how to produce and complete projects successfully. She is passionate about her work, displayed by the volume of her output and research.

As an entertainer, she has toured the world, up for multiple GRAMMY Awards in both her solo acts and group acts. She loves incorporating multi-media in all her events, whether music or speaking, in her seamless presentations. Give her a microphone and a keyboard and you'll experience her deft ability to move between an impactful message and music. There are only a handful of women in the world with her abilities, and only one with her heart and smile: Deborah Johnson.

ALSO BY DEBORAH JOHNSON

BOOKS
Bad Code
Stuck is Not a Four-Letter Word
Music for Kids
Walking with the Hymns: A Devotional Guide
My Father's Favorite Hymns: A Piano-Vocal Music Book

MUSICALS
Tsarina: Book, Music and Lyrics
Stiltz: Music and Lyrics
One Little Kiss: Book, Music and Lyrics

MUSIC ALBUMS
Wayfarer's Journey
The Hero Inside
My Father's Favorite Hymns
Office #7 (Stiltz the Musical)
Double Grandé Experience: Broadway to Hollywood
(with Wayland Pickard)
Classics Rock (Double Grandé with Wayland Pickard)
Tsarina the Musical
Chocolate Songs of Love
One Little Kiss the Musical
Musical Moments
Merry Christmas Too
Classical Spice
Destiny
Single Song Releases Digitally
Many selections of Sheet Music on SheetMusicPlus.com

ENDNOTES

1. Michael Morgenstern, "Automation and Anxiety," *Economist.com*, (June 25, 2016), *https://www.economist.com/news/special-report/21700758-will-smarter-machines-cause-mass-unemployment-automation-and-anxiety*

2. "Stelvio Pass," *Wikipedia, the Free Encyclopedia*, (1988-2018), *https://en.wikipedia.org/wiki/Stelvio_Pass*

3. "The Adventures of Superman," *Supermansupersite.com*, *http://www.supermansupersite.com/1950adventures.html*

4. "Mont Blanc Cable Car Break Threatens Summer Season," Connexion.com, (Jan. 9, 2018), *https://www.connexionfrance.com/French-news/Mont-Blanc-cable-car-break-threatens-summer-season*
Also watch: https://youtu.be/I6UGj9aWCnU

5. "Steve Raible on Wayne Cody and Keith Jackson," *YouYube.com*, *https://youtu.be/83e8Cp9RjVs*

6. Deborah Johnson, "Six Steps to Become a Victim," *YouTube.com*, *https://youtu.be/Y24NG9asBw0*

7. "Shaun White wins Third Snowboard Halfpipe Gold with Nerveless Final Run," *TheGuardian.com*, (Feb. 13, 2018), *https://www.theguardian.com/sport/2018/feb/13/shaun-white-snowboard-halfpipe-gold-scotty-james*

8. David Wharton, "Shaun White's Journey to the Olympics was almost Halted by a Gruesome Injury," *LaTimes.com*, (Feb. 10, 2018), *http://www.latimes.com/sports/olympics/la-sp-olympics-shaun-white-20180210-story.html*

9. Deborah Johnson, *Bad Code: Overcoming Bad Mental Code that Sabotages Your Life* (Upland: DJWorks, 2016), p.111

10. Philip Simmons, *Learning to Fall: The Blessings of an Imperfect Life*, (New York: Bantam, 2003), p.23.

11. Alita Byrd, "World Authority on Laughter Talks Us Through Research," SpectrumMagazine.org, (August 2015), *https://spectrummagazine.org/article/2015/08/09/world-authority-laughter-talks-us-through-research*

12. Louann Brizendine, M.D. *The Female Brain* (New York: Harmony, 2007), Chapter 5, p. 97.
13. Brizendine, Chapter 7, p. 136.
14. Johnson, *Bad Code*
15. "Family Business Facts," FamilyBusinessCenter.com, *http://www.familybusinesscenter.com/resources/family-business-facts/*
16. Charles Duhigg, *The Power of Habit* (New York: Random House, 2012), p.19.
17. "The North Face: Alex Honnold-El Sendero Luminoso," YouTube.com, *https://www.youtube.com/watch?v=Phl82D57P58&app=desktop*
18. Sally Hogshead, *How the World Sees You: Discover Your Highest Value Through the Science of Fascination* (New York: Harper Business, 2014)
19. Isabel Briggs Myers, Peter B. Byers, *Gifts Differing* (Mountain View: Davies-Black, 1980, 1995), p.153.
20. Laura Schocker, "Super Successful Introverts," *HuffingtonPost.com*, (updated Dec. 6, 2017), *https://www.huffingtonpost.com/2015/08/15/famous-introverts_n_3733400.html*
21. Paulette Cohn, "Sunday With Josh Groban," *Parade Magazine*, (Sept. 16, 2018), p.3.
22. Paul D. Tieger, Barbara Barron, *Do What You Are: Discover the Perfect Career* (New York: Little Brown and Company, 2014), p.97
23. "American Generation Fast Facts," *CNN.com*, (Aug. 27, 2017), *https://www.cnn.com/2013/11/06/us/baby-boomer-generation-fast-facts/index.html*
24. *KornFerry.com*, (March 4, 2016), *https://www.kornferry.com/press/new-research-shows-women-are-better-at-using-soft-skills-crucial-for-effective-leadership*
25. Daniel Goleman and Richard E. Goyatzis, "Emotional Intelligence Has 12 Elements. Which do you Need to Work On?" *HarvardBusinessReview.org*, (February 6, 2017), *https://hbr.org/2017/02/emotional-intelligence-has-12-elements-which-do-you-need-to-work-on*
26. Daniel Goleman, Richard Boyatzis and Annie McKee, *Primal Leadership: Unleashing the Power of Emotional Intelligence* (Harvard Business Review Press, 2013)
27. Lahey, Kegan, *Immunity to Change*, p.47.

28 Harriet Tubman (born Araminta Harriet Ross), an African-American abolitionist, humanitarian and Union spy during the American Civil War, (1820-1913).

29 Harriet Tubman, *brainyquote.com*, accessed June 3, 2013, *http://www.brainyquote.com/quotes/quotes/h/harriettub310306.html*.

30 "Shirley Temple," *Wikepedia, the free encyclopedia*, *https://en.wikipedia.org/wiki/Shirley_Temple*

31 "Welcome to the Franchise 500," *Entrepreneur Magazine*, January-February 2018, p.66.

32 "The Future of Jobs: Employment, Skills and Workforce Strategy for the Fourth Industrial Revolution," (January 2016), *http://www3.weforum.org/docs/WEF_FOJ_Executive_Summary_Jobs.pdf*, p.1.

33 Joshua K. Hartshorne, Laura T. Germine, "When Does Cognitive Functioning Peak? The Asynchronous Cognitive Abilities Across the Life Span," *Psychological Science*, (March 13, 2015), http://journals.sagepub.com/doi/abs/10.1177/0956797614567339

34 Anne Trafton, "The Rise and Fall of Cognitive Skills," *MIT News*, (March 6, 2015), *http://news.mit.edu/2015/brain-peaks-at-different-ages-0306*

35 *Future of Jobs*, p.1.

36 Richard N. Bolles, *What Color is Your Parachute? 2018 Edition* (New York: 10 Speed Press, 2018), p.5.

37 "Welcome to the Franchise 500: McDonalds," *Entrepreneur Magazine* January-February 2018, p.70.

38 John Kinde, The Rule of Three: A Humor Technique from the World of Comedy," *HumorPower.com*, *http://www.humorpower.com/art-rulethree.html*

39 Malcom Gladwell, *Outliers: The Story of Success*, (New York: Little Brown and Company, 2008)

40 Greg McKeown, *Essentialism: The Disciplined Pursuit of Less* (New York: Crown Publishing Group, 2014), p. 240.

41 Cal Newport, *So Good They Can't Ignore You*, (New York: Business Plus, 2012), p. 39.

42 "The 100 Best Jobs," USNews.com, (2018), *https://money.usnews.com/careers/best-jobs/rankings/the-100-best-jobs*

43 Catherine Clifford, "5 Daily Habits Olympian Michael Phelps Swears By," *CNBC.com*, Feb. 16, 2017), *https://www.cnbc.com/2017/02/16/5-habits-michael-phelps-developed-that-made-him-a-winner.html*

44 Steven Pressfield, *The War of Art: Break Through the Blocks and Win Your Inner Creative Battles* (New York: Black Irish Entertainment, 2002), p.21.

45 Timothy Ferriss, *The 4-Hour Workweek* (New York: Crown Publishing, 2009)

46 *Speaker Magazine,* 12.4, Dec. 2017, p.35-37.

47 Lisa Laskow Lahey, Robert Kegan, *Immunity to Change* (Boston: Harvard Business School), p.39.

48 Charles, Duhigg, *The Power of Habit* (New York: Random House, 2014), p.95.

49 Duhigg, p. 32-35.

50 "Why Electronics may Stimulated You Before Bed," *SleepFoundation.org,* 2018, https://sleepfoundation.org/sleep-topics/why-electronics-may-stimulate-you-bed

51 "The State of American Dining in 2016," *Zagat.com, https://www.zagat.com/b/the-state-of-american-dining-in-2016*

52 "2018 Physical Activity Guidelines Advisory Committee Scientific Report," *health.gov,* (2018), *https://health.gov/paguidelines/second-edition/report/pdf/PAG_Advisory_Committee_Report.pdf,* p. F9-6.

53 Mark S. Greenberg, Kaloyan Taney, Marie-France Marin, Roger K. Pitman, "Stress, PTSD, and Dementia," *alzheimersanddementia.com,* Vol. 10, Issue 3, Supplement, Pages S155-S165, (June 2014), *https://www.alzheimersanddementia.com/article/S1552-5260(14)00136-8/fulltext*

54 Johnson, *Bad Code,* p.145-6.

55 Ananya Mandal, MD, "New Brain Cells are added in Elderly Adult Brains Too," *news-medical.net,* (April 6, 2018), *https://www.news-medical.net/news/20180406/New-brain-cells-are-added-in-elderly-adult-brains-too.aspx*

56 Shannon Davis, "Traveling on a Rope Team," *climbing.com,* (Feb. 24, 2014), *https://www.climbing.com/skills/traveling-on-a-rope-team/*

57 Toni Fitzgerald, "Royal Wedding Ratings: How Many People Watched Prince Harry Wed Meghan Markle?" *forbes.com,* (May 21, 2018), *https://www.forbes.com/sites/tonifitzgerald/2018/05/21/royal-wedding-ratings-how-many-people-watched-prince-harry-wed-meghan-markle/#4994b35d55c6*

58. Ruberman W, Weinblatt E, Goldberg JD, Chaudhary BS, "Psychosocial Influences on Mortality after Myocardial Infarction," *ncbi.nlm,nih.gov,* (Aug. 30, 1984), *https://www.ncbi.nlm.nih.gov/pubmed/6749228*

59. N. Scarmeas, G. Levy, M.X. Tang and Y. Stern, "Influence of Leisure Activity on the Incidence of Alzheimer's Disease," *Neurology 57,* no. 12 (2001): 2236-42.

60. Gary Chapman, *The Five Love Languages: The Secret to Love That Lasts,* (Chicago, Northfield, 2015)

61. Norma Deloris Egstrom (May 26, 1920-January 21,2002) known professionally as Peggy Lee, was an American jazz and popular music singer, songwriter, composer and actress.

62. Susan David, The Gift and Power of Emotional Courage," ted.com, (2017), *https://www.ted.com/talks/susan_david_the_gift_and_power_of_emotional_courage/transcript?utm_source=tedcomshare&utm_medium=email&utm_campaign=tedspread*

63. "Change Quotes," *brainyquote.com, https://www.brainyquote.com/topics/change*

64. Bernard Marr, "9 Technology Mega Trends that will Change the World in 2018,:, forbes.com, (Dec. 3, 2017), *https://www.forbes.com/sites/bernardmarr/2017/12/04/9-technology-mega-trends-that-will-change-the-world-in-2018/#4718515b5eed*

65. Behe, Michael J., *Darwin's Black Box,* Free Press, New York, NY, 1996, 2006, p.42.

66. "Touching Moments from Billy Graham's Funeral," *youtube.com,* (March 3, 2018), *https://www.youtube.com/watch?v=YkJB9-rfuc4,* Quote by Billy Graham at 3:24.

www.ingramcontent.com/pod-product-compliance
Lightning Source LLC
Chambersburg PA
CBHW050639300426
44112CB00012B/1860